YORK

YORK

ARCHAEOLOGICAL WALKING GUIDES

CLIFFORD JONES

The History Press

Publisher's Note

The views expressed herein are those of the author
and do not necessarily represent those of the publisher.

Front cover image: York Walls and war memorial, Station Road, York, England.

First published 2012

The History Press
The Mill, Brimscombe Port
Stroud, Gloucestershire, GL5 2QG
www.thehistorypress.co.uk

Reprinted 2017

British Library Cataloguing in Publication Data.
A catalogue record for this book is available from the British Library.

ISBN 978 0 7524 6524 1

Typesetting and origination by The History Press
Printed in Great Britain

CONTENTS

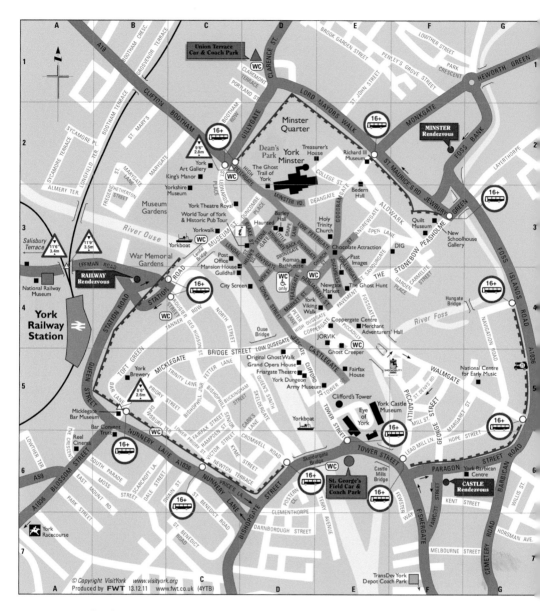

Map of York. *Courtesy of www.visityork.org*

PROLOGUE

York is a place of enlightenment, religiosity and no little serenity. It is an important commercial hub and retains excellent links with mainland Europe; it is a powerful force across the north of Britain and further afield. It is a substantial historic point on the map; a place for anyone with determination, skills and no little wit to hone a reputation on an international stage.

So thought the scholar Alcuin, who taught in the great post-Roman seat of learning at York in the eighth century and went on to work for the Holy Roman Emperor, Carolus Magnus, better known as Charlemagne (714–842). York had been on the European stage for over 600 years at the time and has remained so ever since. The religiosity may have taken a hit over the centuries, and the power may have peaked and waned, but York is still a magnificent city and draws the world to its door.

York is a good place to be at any time.

This guide is not for those looking for a gentle and all-encompassing 'hold my hand and lead me' guide around York; it is for those whom wish for a deeper experience, those that wish to gain a better understanding of the sense of place and time. Just like archaeology, which to the author is the art of seeking the past with as many of the facts to set him upon the path of exploration as possible. And then by the finding of the actual, the stone, pot and tooth of the matter; discovering (with no great surprise as is happens every time) that what was taken as fact turns out to be quite different or completely wrong in the actual, sending a train of debate in yet another direction – it is always a surprise and to the author always a good one at that.

York and its environs are just the same.

Let the place tell the story in its own way; let it draw you in, it is friendly enough; let it reveal itself in its own time and way. There will be areas of revelation, doubt and interpretation leading to dispute, but that is what pubs are for.

None of the routes around the city are difficult in the physical sense, but many are challenging in respect of the perception and understanding. The way York presents itself is through publicity and marketing blurs some of the edges – and edges are often the most interesting bits.

The author may lead you astray – it is the temperament of the beast. He is liable to 'go off on one', but there is usually method in his rant and direction. The walker will soon get used to his ways. Perhaps York has entered into his soul, as it tends to do.

The very nature of York does not lend itself to pastiche; the solidity of its foundation grafted in time requires a certain amount of respect from any writer and guide. Others may try to sum the place up, but the result will oft as not be a gallop through time with brief glimpses to catch the breath before hurtling through another couple of decades or so. It hardly does justice to the place – it creates a blur upon a furrowed, perplexed brow and rightly deserves better attention from the walker than that.

To summarise what all others will tell: York appeared as a hunting camp by a boat fording point between two rivers, probably a bit of open river bank clear of trees (a result of seasonal flooding), about 7,000 years ago. Time passed, as it is prone to do, and the river became a recognised highway for trade; tribes established themselves and the coming of metal had introduced an order of hierarchy and wealth that needed order and protection. The Romans appeared with their well organized ways; the tribes were subsumed – not just through Roman superiority on the battle field but from internal tribal differences. Rome, having made the spot great, passed the mantle of control to the Anglo-Saxons, who in turn passed it to the Norse then to the Normans. Having been constructed on the remains of the Roman fort by the Angles, the religious importance of the Minster as a symbol of the State remains a dominant feature up to the present day. York carries the weight of responsibility for the north of England, thrives on wool then slumps into obscurity, rises again after the Black Death and sees out a civil war to become the cultural capital of the Georgian north. The coming of the railways offered commercial opportunities and tourism; the flow of time, ever constant, continues and no doubt archaeologists will be digging up bits of tourist buses and cameras from the twenty-first century in the years to come.

Note: the author has endeavoured in his own inimitable way to edit out all mention of ghosts, unnatural phenomenon and the like. There is enough history to York and, as far as the author is concerned, there is as much to interest and indeed shock the walker in the actual as the supernatural can ever offer. So the ghost stories must have made their own way into the text – spooky!

This 'tourismo' summary provides the visitor with York in a nutshell; but not a very interesting nut, no real bite, no texture, rather bland and slight in pith, nothing of the most important component: the people of York and their lives at street level. The people that put the place up, tore it down and put it up again; those that lived and breathed in the streets, traded, loved and died here – and occasionally wandered ever after around the Shambles trying to work out how to get out. They are the most important components of all; the structures rise and fall but the lives of those that inhabited York are the essential glue. That is the true nature of the adventure, understanding and being a part of life in York.

For the purpose of better understanding York, the author politely requests the walker to take the mantle of the man or woman on the street, marching as a Roman soldier or rich Norse trader; as a Royalist with fine plumes and a jaunty gait; a Georgian dandy; railway worker or fireman. Dress up if you wish, you will add to the very fabric of the place and no doubt find the odd coin thrown in your direction!

The walker is not a tourist, but a researcher. Remember this; it comes in useful, especially for those sticky moments when you are questioned as to why you are wherever you maybe and others think you should not be there. There is a variation on this ploy – more anon. The author's alternative to the tourist guide is not to attempt to tell the walker everything; firstly, the author certainly does not know everything about York and would like to meet the soul that does. Secondly, an insight (which this is) to the place and people within it offers a field of research and research leads to personal fulfilment, which, to the author's mind, is both a pleasure and leisure. The key word here is leisure; this is supposed to be fun. So start enjoying it. That's an order. There is nothing better than the personal satisfaction of discovery; it gives one a tingle up the spine and gets the hairs standing upright, and leads on to new and unexpected lands.

Exploration and research has to be disciplined, but has its truly enthralling rewards. This guide is for those that like to dip deep into the pool of life and fish out something new and carry away a scintilla of the lives of those that lived in York – if the walker manages that, the author has done his job well enough.

This guide is more a signpost than anything else; imagination and observation are essential – there is much to put back together that has long gone, but it's worth the effort. The author has always believed that the best way to explore anywhere is to dive in and enjoy the experiences that come with the splash of contact. This can be a sudden shock to the system and a sharp intake of breath, especially if there is little tangible of the past to see – a leap of faith is required. The author therefore provides the directions and some of the more important clues before setting the walker off on the diverse paths that make up the history of York. The ways around and through York are by no means straight; the whole is bent by the weight of time and oft as not equally distorted by our misinterpretation of it, which only adds to the confusion. The author does his best to straighten things out or at least point out where further information can be gathered.

York is full of hidden corners, not as obvious as the walker may think. The Minster and Shambles are not all of York. The past and its exploration is not unlike a game of three-dimensional chess. The walker will need to have their wits about them to make sense of it all and the author expects that this guide will offer up a desire to find out more – indeed, that is the very purpose. But, that also allows for genuine discovery, which is a wonderful thing – try it and see.

York attracts hundreds of thousands of visitors a year; its Minster and cluster of tightly packed streets have become a synonymous with the present seeking a sensation of the past. The city has benefitted from such interest and serviced the need with gusto; making the most of one's assets is undoubtedly a good thing for those that live and work around York. Getting the balance right between visitor and resident is not always an easy one, but the author has spent many years trundling around the city and, being naturally curious and not adverse to the odd pint in the darker corners of some of the city pubs, has got to know the locals well enough to know that there is a relatively benign feeling between the two. The city needs the visitors to maintain itself; indeed, the visitors contribute greatly towards the upkeep and the discovery of the past. York Archaeology is one of the few units in the UK that can be seen to be thriving in these deeply worrying times; all because it has taken a direct commercial involvement in tourism by offering the visitor a chance to experience archaeology first hand. This accessibility, this openness, is core to York's overall success; it is a place everyone wants to be, because it is genuinely welcoming.

Being busy is part of York's lot; busy equals trade and trade in all its guises is what York is for. It has had its declines, it has seen boom and bust, but it would not be the city it is today without such reminders still staring back at the walker; buildings not replaced because there was no need nor money to do so – time passing them by along with the demolition ball. Survivors from many ages by need, chance and good sense all rub together to make a jumbled whole. This jumble works as a necessity of life, merging centuries across rooftop beams and the very walls of rooms themselves. If the multitudinous parts were disassembled the city would vanish; not one stone or brick would stand upon another. It is this desire to be within an historical architectural presence that draws the crowds.

Perception is the key. The present has many pasts within it and the author will offer up a few key dates for York as focal points; they are not the only ones, but there is a practical need to give some preliminary boundaries if only to get an initial view and thus begin the process of unravelling the city.

The author is all in favour of the walker jumping in any direction they wish: experimentation and experience is no less a discipline, as long as something is learned and the effort recorded, if only with a photograph, because the understanding of the past is a very personal thing – all views are aspects of a whole, hardly ever seen as the same thing, which makes this a very personal challenge.

THE AUTHOR'S MOTTO
GET LOST. IT'S THE ONLY WAY TO TRULY UNDERSTAND ANYWHERE.

The basic formulas are …
- Take time to look – longer than you think. Stop look and listen.
  Take on board the essence of York.
- Look at the relationship of one thing to another and how a sense of place works.
  Strip away the present.
- How, why and when – little words, big questions.
- Never be frightened to ask, most people don't bite.
- Record: pencil, notebook and camera – use them.

There will be ample opportunity to rest and enjoy the delights of food and ale, there being a brewery in the city and as many eateries as you could shake a chicken leg at. The author will touch upon both subjects throughout as he feels it his personal attempt to bolster the York economy by doing so. This guide will provide a balance between belt notch and activity; however, the author will be generous enough to state that in his case the belt notch was loosened in the course of his studious reflections several times – showing the dedication to which he has put his humble frame.

But enough of his exploding shirt buttons.

It is now time to prepare for the adventure ahead.

GETTING STARTED

York is a city that does not require walking boots to tread its streets, nor backpacks, so both can be given a holiday. Good walking shoes suitable for a city, worn in and comfortable are preferable – the author considers 'comfortable' as equating to that very short period between the translucent thickness of leather becoming a very obvious hole; after that the sock will surely follow. Fortunately, with plenty of opportunities to find replacements for both, there is no need to pack a spare pair.

The basic rule is: comfort.

Walking a city does have its considerable advantages and the author's usual list of warnings and assistance are unnecessary in this case, there being a very slim chance for sheep tics to attack.

A useful list for use in an emergency is located at the back of this guide.

Somewhere to keep the necessaries of the day is a must and should include room for a camera, notebook and pencil. This may seem obvious but needs some consideration. Observation should be recorded; digital is fine, but can be a distraction and rightly frowned upon as with much use of mobile phones in most public buildings, including the Minster and museums. A notepad and pencil need no batteries.

SECURITY

York is full of tourists and thus is an attractive proposition to those that would like to relieve the rest of us of our hard-earned funds and possessions. The situation is no more serious than it is anywhere else, just take sensible precautions: keep things zipped up, out of view or locked in your hotel safe.

The great advantage of York is that nowhere is very far from the starting point. Allow for some retail therapy, which should not interfere with

York train station – the only way to properly arrive

Easy-to-follow bus destination boards

exploration, because a contrast can bring details into sharper view. Any of the walks can be interrupted as needs must. When it comes to retail therapy, the author realises he is an exception: he goes out to shop only for what is needed and nothing else – out and straight back and is none too amused (it is difficult at the best of times to amuse him) when retailers move things around in the aisles. York is a city for specialist shops, proper customer service and a level of care and attention found in few other places.

The other great advantage of York is if it turns a tad inclement there is always a place of warmth and comfort available, and whilst the streets don't stop the rain, there is no shortage of places to avoid it.

Unless funds are critical there is no need to carry food with you; there is no shortage of places to dine at any reasonable hour. York is blessed with some excellent restaurants, bistros, cafes and pubs. There are certain exceptional establishments that only serve local fare and the author can do no more than encourage the walker to seek them out and experience them to the full as often as is possible.

NAVIGATION

A map might also help, of course.

The walker can obtain a map of York; this is not difficult to do. A simple one without too much detail is best, just to allow the walker to know which way is north is enough; it would spoil the fun otherwise. There are many versions of maps and even downloads. The major problem is trying to relate the maps to the actual place, especially in the more compressed areas of York. The author knows only too well that on any day of the year there will be little groups of visitors staring, spinning and arguing over a map. After a little while, the group will curse the thing, shove it into a pocket and head with determination, oft as not, in the wrong direction – the author only surmises the wrong direction as the group will reappear at the same spot within a few minutes and then head off with as much gusto as before in the opposite direction. This process can continue for some time until the group gets smaller, members having been lost along the way or have determined upon independence of purpose and sallied forth on another course alone.

The whole city is best managed along the lines of, what is within the walls doesn't really need anything more than common sense. North of the river is the Minster; south of the river is the railway station. As the author says, 'Getting lost is the thing!'

GETTING STARTED

The walks start at points that can be found by following the plentiful signposts, which, very sensibly, York city provides. It is pointless offering timescales as the walker will no doubt be sidetracked along the way. If not, the walker is making a serious mistake – stop, start again and do it properly!

GETTING ABOUT: JUST GET OUT THERE AND WALK

There are buses in York and they do come in useful; the walker will enjoy the use of them. Fortunately, York is relatively car free; it could be improved, but overall the situation is much better than in many cities. There are some awkward pinch points where pedestrians and traffic come together, but just use the pedestrian crossings and all will be well.

At the time of writing, First Group control the majority of services within York city centre. They have a very useful map available via www.firstgroup. com/ukbus/york/assets/pdfs/maps/york_city_centre_map.pdf.

There is an excellent set of bus services from outside the railway station and reasonable signage as to where one catches what and how often.

TERMINOLOGY

A bar is a formal gateway through the walls of the city; basically, they would have barred access, hence bar. The bars are Micklegate, Bootham, Monk, Walmgate, Fishergate and Victoria. The word 'gate' is from the Norse *gata*, meaning way. Ginnel is a passageway between buildings. The word snicket also applies to a narrow passageway and has transmuted within York to snikelways as a result of the excellent little work, *A Walk Around the Snickelways of York* by M.W. Jones. Snickets tend to be public rights of way.

ACCESS

York in general has good accessibility save for the city walls, which can be hard going, even for the author, with steep steps, narrow passages and in places none too even surfaces.

York has an excellent access guide: www.york.gov.uk/content/45053/ 64897/133965/city_centre_access.pdf.

WEATHER

York is well known for its fog and mist. As expected for a city by two rivers, it also has a reputation for floods and in recent years these have been severe. July and August are typically the warmest, which comes as no surprise, and December and March are perishing cold and frosty. Snow has been known of recent years, which looks wonderful until it freezes on the pavements in ankle-breaking icebergs. The author finds pre-Christmas a grand time to visit; York knows how to play its Dickensian street hand to the limit – why not, if you've got it, flaunt it! Whilst the winter days are short, the atmosphere is wonderful. A winter visit to York can be exhilarating, but on occasions more than a little damp; the advantages being a sense of having the city to oneself and there being plenty of places to warm the bones.

In fact, any time of year is fine, but try to avoid bank holidays and the Ebor Festival at the Races (unless you wish to combine archaeology with a flutter on the horses), which can make accommodation hard to come by.

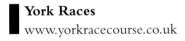

York Races
www.yorkracecourse.co.uk

ACCOMMODATION

Booking your accommodation well in advance is of primary importance. As to cost, the author suggests a very rough rule of thumb. The closer to the centre of the city, the more expensive the accommodation; however, this also includes some fantastic very private, managed apartments hidden away from the more boisterous and rumbustious stews. Seek these very exclusive places to rest. There will be a sizeable cost, but one very much worth paying for the quality.

The glory of York is that there really is somewhere for every pocket.

THE WALKS

WALK 1

ON THE ROAD

- **Starting point: Micklegate Bar**
- **Starting time: 9 a.m. at the very latest**

This will be a challenging walk, not because of terrain, but, being the earliest period covered, it is the deepest from the physical gaze. However, it provides a foundation for all that comes after and thus is an essential stage. It highlights the enormous physical impact that the Romans had and the effective establishment of York. While there was native occupation of the area it is utterly subsumed by the Roman shovel.

SETTING THE SCENE

It is AD 72 and the Roman army is making its sweaty, disciplined and mud-splattered way along the newly constructed road to the new fort at Eboracum (York). Forget the MGM version of the Roman army, it would have marched well enough but it would have looked dusty and rough round the edges with the sweet mixture of sweat, vinegar and rancid fish oil (delicious stuff)

19

escorted by a few swarms of flies trying to dine on the day's recently dispatched meat ration. The IX Legion Hispana had been extremely busy in the previous year under their commander Petilius Cerealis, who, taking advantage of internal strife within the Brigante tribe, had taken the initiative to move the Roman military establishment in Britannia further north to this new forward stronghold, Eboracum. Any advance needs a back-up and supply line; indeed, most of the military effort is not in the fighting of an enemy but the supply machinery behind the front line. The Romans, with typical efficiency and engineering prowess, had constructed a magnificent new road from Lindum Colonia (York), which was an extension of the road from London now known as Ermine Street, to do just that. There is good reason to believe that the course of this road does take some cognisance of earlier tribal pathways but ploughs straight through any boundaries or habitation – making it clear that the diplomacy of the past was just that, the past.

The IX Legion now march on with a quickening of pace as rest is close at hand; down the hill to the river and the new, if somewhat temporary, bridge.

Eboracum in AD 72 would still smell of wood resin, the structure of the fort would not be completely finished, the ditches around it on the far bank of the Ouse would still be very sharp and clean, a good deal of mud would be lingering and piles of gravels would be still waiting to be spread to assist in laying down additional cobbled ways. The tile kilns down by the River Foss would still be busy, clay still being dug in pits a short distance from the river edge, indicating earlier courses of the ancient river bed. The tiles produced would proudly be stacked up with the legion stamp on them; they would be awaiting the completion of the carpenter's work on the barrack roofs. The problem with the tiles was their weight; they would need hefty timbers. The timber walls of the fort would have already shown some signs of movement; those to the east were in need of attention and those facing the river to the south were likewise exposed to some adverse conditions. The one advantage of timber is an element of flexibility, but maintenance was always going to be high. The turf banking would have assisted in the short term, but when it dried out it would crumble away and lose its stability.

All this work was seen as the initial stage of occupation; any locals would be stunned by the efficiency and the unification (and the smell of fish oil) – disciplined design, disciplined display of military might; just as effective at quelling any opposition as the sword. An atmosphere of control pervaded; personal passion for freedom on the part of any local tribes would have been easily quashed, although most would have seen the Romans as an opportunity and one that would come to last for over 300 years.

The Roman fort road lies some metres below the street seen here

Cerealis, having established the site, had moved on at a terrifying speed, crossing the country and eventually heading for Carlisle across what would have been a suicidal pathway had not the Brigante tribe been a divided people. In one daring year, Cerealis laid down the possibility for Roman control of the land to the south of the Tyne and Solway. It would take some years to develop the expansion and Agricola to do his part, but the core factor was the establishment of York: supply base, trade centre and a beacon of Roman establishment.

Eboracum, or *Eburaci*, is translated as 'the place of the yew trees.' Yew trees are very fussy as to where they will thrive and do not tolerate soggy conditions; this is significant and the author wonders if the translation requires a bit of a rethink, as the Roman fort at York lies on the Ouse with the Foss as its immediate neighbour. It is notable that two temporary forts have been discovered just 2.5km further north from the outskirts of York at Bootham Stray, which suggests that the initial military consideration was to protect the Ouse river crossing in depth by having a forward base clear of the crossing, deliberately encroaching on a tribal boundary and giving room to bring up additional forces across the river crossing rather than at it. These

The majestic River Ouse

forward camps allowed for the establishment of York in AD 71. These camps lie at SE598548280 and SE596548, though they are best viewed from the air. Whilst they are minor in scale to York, they indicate intensive military presence at an early stage of Roman occupation, probably in reaction to the Brigante civil war.

Early transients wandering along the riverbanks of what ultimately became York would have thus found themselves paddling through a couple of millennia of soggy river bank before the Romans turned up. The author is keen to use the word 'transient' as there is little evidence of early permanent residency of what was to become York. A hoard of Neolithic axes (you can see them in the museum) seems more likely booty that had been buried, but nonetheless evidence of hunting parties working up and down the river and camping at a convenient fishing point exists (a situation that seems not to have changed much, if at all), right through to the arrival of the Romans.

The Romans had a strict military policy of guarding river crossings, both for security and tax collection, and as Cerealis was undertaking a major military campaign, the Ouse would have been seen as a major crossing point. The fort was established on the north bank, which indicates determined long-term control over a natural, recognised boundary. The opportunity for delivery of supplies up the River Ouse would have been a decisive factor in establishing York; the new bridge across the Ouse would act as a terminus to a large river and maritime craft at this point. Military supplies and, of course, general trade acts as a magnet to all parties. Trade established itself wherever the Romans went: bars, brothels, leather and metalworkers appear as if by magic, as well as the odd temple and all the basic needs of life; if the fort becomes established the wife and kids might turn up as well.

Enough wittering; the author is keen to get started and trust, the walker is too!

Find Micklegate Bar, south of the river to the south-east of the railway station. The walker should be standing on the outside of the city wall at

WALK 1

GENERAL RULE

THE WALKER SHOULD ASK IF THEY ARE LOST; PEOPLE ARE GENERALLY NICE, DON'T BITE AND TRY TO BE HELPFUL.

Micklegate Bar – the bar of at least twelfth-century origin and a site that is worthy of note and visit. However, it is not of Roman origin, except for bits of reused Roman masonry, and it is not the site of the Roman road entering the approach to the early fort. Time and circumstance along with the earth worm have done their work.

There. The walker has started and the first thing physically surveyed is not what is supposed to be viewed at all; the walker will get into the way the author introduces the city as the walks go on!

Micklegate is the city's welcoming statement for travellers from the south. In AD 1196 permission from the Crown was granted to build a sophisticated gate structure, suggesting the city had enough spare monies to advertise its worth. By the fifteenth century, the structure was further enhanced to include the opportunity to advertise loyalty to the Crown by displaying the butchered remains of any miscreant that might come to hand. So Micklegate can be seen as an advertising board, 'Welcome to York – see what happens if you steal the hotel towels'. All jolly good stuff!

The spot beyond Micklegate Bar is a busy one. The ring road at the crossroads can be a noisy spot, which is at divergence with its name, Blossom Street, suggestive of orchards. It is not, it is a transmutation of the word *Ploxwangate*, 'street of the ploughs mender', which gives the walker some idea of how the English language is and continues to be a flexible one.

The Roman road is nowhere to be seen here, but if you walk out to the crossroads and turn right on to Queens Street and line up the taxi offices with the city wall, this is roughly the line of the Roman road from Petuaria (Brough by Humber) heading down towards Eboracum. It is to be noted that in the driest of summers the grass dries out fastest where the ancient road surface lies closest to the present ground surface, which is the top of the *agger* (the raised mass of the road; the *nucleus* being the road surface, which can be compacted gravel, paving, concrete or cobble depending on the availability of material and where the road is – in towns, paving and cobble). Under this lay the *rudus*, a sand and gravel layer giving the strength, and beneath that the *statument* consisting of the base layer or layers of stone set in clay (where available); the *statument* is the flat, wide section of the *fossa* dug to provide the road width and the ditches on either side. The author has noted many Roman roads by the two ditches, as in dry weather they remain green longest. Allowing for the present gardening and the building and removal of structures over the centuries, there is still some evidence that the ditches here work as there are some trees close to the left-side ditch; there are three, all planted at the same time – note which two have grown to be the largest.

There is no pervading smell of sweat and rancid fish.

The grass bank and stone city wall is a much restored one. This is not a new process; the Romans constructed a gate here (in the late first century), to allow access to their walled colony. It would have had two entrances with towers on either side and would have been far more substantial than Micklegate, which, to be fair, is an effective barrier and an excellent weapons platform in its own right. A very impressive site even at the start, probably the highest structure the locals had ever seen, and in the next three centuries it would become a veritable skyscraper with potentially three floors.

The walker, being unable to go through the bank and stone, should head back through the Micklegate Bar and turn immediately left into Bar Lane; walk to the corner and turn right, which leads on to the Roman road. In AD 72 this would have been open fields; much would change in the coming years but in the early Roman occupation of the area this would still have only been the site of a few roadside shanties providing refreshments and foodstuffs, perhaps tented encampments with cattle and horses, and traders doing business with the Roman army. This mishmash of people could be the remnants of a native settlement, a *canabae* – the Roman description of native self-managing communities. The Brigantes were by AD 71 a broken tribe; the 'high ones' had fallen very low after two disastrous civil wars.

There was a series of early Roman buildings, some quite sophisticated, 50m from the new road a little further south of Micklegate at the Mount. These were never modernised and the site abandoned any further building in later Roman periods. It is possible that these related to the Brigantes' client kingdom status, and once that was dead and gone the Romans would have had no reason to renew the site. See http://ads.ahds.ac.uk/catalogue/search/fr.cfm?rcn=YATGAZ-1991.4&m=1.

This commercial activity would be formalised in the future, but for the time being it was a haphazard arrangement. One feature has not changed; the need for refreshment. York Brewery stands proudly on the route and is a welcome site on what is now Toft Green.

York Brewery offer tours, which the author thoroughly recommends.

York Brewery
12 Toft Green
York, YO1 6JT
Tel: 01904 621 162
Fax: 01904 621 216
Email: enquiries@york-brewery.co.uk

Toft Green, on the left-hand side, is the site of the first railway station in York, a terminus station, where the lines were built through the city walls. The walker will be visiting the railway age later in the guide. So if anything is missed on this walk do not fear, a return is inevitable. The author muses that the area has always been involved with transport and commerce for York, with the delivery of goods and visitors from the very beginning – a true gateway.

The walker should proceed down Toft Green, which falls away from the level on which the station remains standing to the left. Toft Green becomes without warning Tanners Row, giving a clear indication of the area's use.

The author wonders if the tanners (post-Roman era) had discovered the grand bathhouse hereabouts and converted its remains into tanning basins. The smell in this part of the city must have been interesting.

Cross the junction of Rougier Street and George Hudson Street (the great, if flawed, railway entrepreneur) at the crossroads, then head down the second part of Tanners Row. The buildings begin to become obviously more ancient in nature; everything to this point has (save for Micklegate and parts of the city wall) been no more than 250 years old – at the junction of Tanners Row with Wellington Row (left) and North Street (right) the buildings are of a much earlier date and worthy of further investigation, especially the tearooms.

Toft Green – the redevelopment of the old railway

North Street

Archaeological research on Wellington Row has revealed its potential pre-Roman usage: evidence of a turf bank that may be associated with a cattle enclosure or, alternatively, a basic flood defence for a settlement which included stock corralling has been noted. The area has clear indication of butchery throughout the Roman occupation. The river would have run red with the blood – a pleasant thought. See www.york.ac.uk/inst/chumpal/EAU-reps/EAU95-14.pdf.

For the purposes of the walker's experience of early Roman York, these archaeological findings suggest that the Roman road acted as a linear settlement for some considerable distance. It should also be noted that the name of the roads indicate the continuing understanding of their usage over the millennia.

The Roman road is slightly to the left of the present T-junction at this point and crosses into the small garden by the River Ouse. Here there would have been a timber gateway with sentry towers and a great wooden bridge across the river, and on the far side the formidable bulk of the *castra* (fort).

The walker should take close note of the far bank; the Guildhall (much restored after the Luftwaffe did some creative remodelling) the bridge came ashore just between the highest point of the Guildhall (at this point) and its junction with the lower, roofed part. The author believes the Guildhall juts out into the Ouse at a slight angle as a result of the builders finding the remains of the foundations of the slightly later Roman stone bridge's erosion defences. The original bridge would have required constant maintenance and would have suffered greatly with the extremes of the Ouse and the seasons.

The walker should walk along Wellington Row and take the left turn into Tanners Moat to take a few moments to reflect on what has been seen so far. Head to the Maltings for a welcoming spot of light refreshment.

The Maltings
Postern Tower
Tanner's Moat
York YO1 6HU
Tel: 01904 655 387

The author hopes the walker has been able to strip everything of the present away; this is a very difficult first test for the walker. The only dominating feature in York in AD 72 would be the fort and the bridge; all else would be a rather haphazard semi-rural, noisy, smelly mess. The sense of impact on this glacial moraine washed by two rivers with the odd bit of forestry would

have been quite incredible – that was the point, the visual impact of military discipline, organisation and administration being big and flashy all play their part in Roman occupation; it's a mental thing, not just a physical one.

The road, now buried deep beneath the bustle of York, would have been a dramatic incursion, not just into the land, but into the very soul of those whose land it had been. There is a direct relationship between the building of Roman roads in Britannia and the building of the great inter-continental railways in the Americas. The impact was ultimately devastating to the close-knit tribal structure.

The walker will have also noted that parts of the walk so far are through the slightly more workman-like bits of York; it is not part of any recognised tourist routes (excluding Micklegate environs), which is because others think there isn't a great deal to see. How wrong they are.

Having enjoyed the delights of the Maltings, proceed up Tanners Moat to Station Road, which is a really busy spot for traffic; cross the pedestrian crossings and turn right on to Thomas Page's superb engineering triumph of 1863, Lendal Bridge. The arch is an absolutely stunning piece of Victorian engineering. The Romans would have been equally impressed.

The Maltings, Lendal Bridge

WALK 1

Cross over the bridge and turn left into the York Museum Gardens. These botanic gardens are York's lungs; the grass is oft as not covered by office workers and mothers with children enjoying the space. In an age of digital stimulation, it is joyous to see that the simple delights of looking at flowers and sitting on grass in the sun are still able to hold their own. The gardens, designed by Sir John Naysmith in the 1830s on behalf of the Yorkshire Philosophical Society, incorporate the medieval ruins of St Mary's abbey and St Leonard's chapel, and the not to be missed Yorkshire Museum.

▐ Yorkshire Museum
www.yorkshiremuseum.org.uk/Page/Index.aspx

However, for the purpose of this walk the most important feature is the western corner of the Roman fort. The structure the walker is faced with is the later stone fort's corner. It is a sophisticated piece of work, the Multangular Tower, a ten-sided tower. It is the only standing survivor of eight built on the walls of the fort as part of the rebuilding of the defences during Emperor Septimus Severus' campaign in the north in AD 209–11. So these remains didn't exist in AD 72 when we started our walk.

In AD 72 there would have been a wooden tower at the corner and a goodly sized and deep defensive ditch. No doubt there would have been a group of Roman soldiers arguing over how effective the *fossa fastigata* (the ankle breaker) in the bottom of the defensive ditch was supposed to be and whether it was more use as a means of keeping the water level down, the Romans having fully understood that the river was rather too close for comfort.

There would have been a road avoiding the fort, following its western side, reconnecting with the northern road from the fort heading for Newcastle-upon-Tyne. The fort was a military establishment; commerce and general traffic went around rather than interfering with the running of the day-to-day life of the Roman army. Passing within the fort's gaze, nobody could claim anonymity in this space; as open spaces, roads made for good killing zones.

The walker now has a corner and to archaeologists corners are really useful, especially when it comes to Roman forts; the standardisation of *castra* (land reserved for military defensive purposes) are such that dimensions can be estimated. However, in this case estimation is not required; the fort and centre of administration thrived and the site remains in use to this day. This is not to say there was no alteration, even in the first two centuries of Roman control a great deal of rebuilding of the fort was required, but the line of the later stone walls act as a good ground plan to the earlier wooden fort, which survived until

Bootham Bar

AD 108. Up to then, original timbers and turf construction had been replaced with a more sound clay mound and oak-timbered structure during the campaigns of Agricola.

Archaeological excavations on Coney Street identified that the original fortification was of a wooden palisade on a bank approximately 6m wide, made of clay from the river, with oak strips acting as a binding and turf as a cover for the clay against the weather. The wooden wall would be no more than 4m high.

The walker will now commence a journey of understanding, or bewilderment, of the scale of Roman military power and administration. The road towards the fort has been followed, indeed the walker has stayed exactly on the road's path as it diverts around the fort, but it is time to make a foray

Bootham Art Gallery

York bus tours

around its perimeter. The walker should take the path from the Multangular Tower towards the Yorkshire Museum building, but turn right before it and head down the side of the building, with the city wall on the right. The walker may like to pace out the distance; the destination is Bootham Bar, which will appear to the right, heralded by some rather grand buildings on the way. York Art Gallery is worthy of an excursion and sitting by the fountain is a must in summer for a cooling spray. The York tour buses leave from here and there is always a gaggle of tour guides trying to tempt you aboard; it is worth the fare – if only to sit down and enjoy the view.

Bootham Bar is the only entrance to the city of York precisely on the site of an original Roman fort entrance, the *Porta Principalis*. The entrance the walker is looking at is a good metre above that of the entrance of AD 72 – the subsequent deliberate destruction and reconstruction as well as the general debris of life over the centuries has seen all of York rise considerably. If the walker was strolling along in AD 72 the body would be well below the present-day surface.

The view in AD 72 would have been somewhat different to the chunky stone block adorned with late medieval firing platforms and later folly adornments. The walker would be looking at something more akin to a 'Wild West' fort entrance with a simple platform above. Indeed, the whole fort would look very like that; Cerealis was in far too much of a hurry to have his troops consider anything more substantial. The need for a safe base to work from

Reflections on the Ouse

comes higher on the list than the need for immediate permanency, and if you are in a hurry and need a base you go for standardised design which your troops are well versed in constructing. There are only so many shapes and techniques anyone can use, especially when working with wood. The author considers the analogy with the American cavalry construction and the Roman army a fair one – at least it gives the walker a 'view' of what this earliest stage looked like, which is very different from what came later and what is standing on the same spot to this day.

The walker should cross the road, using the pedestrian crossing. Head for the bar, enter and head up to the wall walk. Bootham Bar still has its portcullis, installed to keep armies and rioters (York having had one or two disagreeable moments over the centuries) from getting on to High Petergate.

In the summer the walls can be crowded, hence the suggestion of an early start on this walk – best to do the walls without the crowds that can seriously delay the day, the walls being naturally built for defence, not hordes of tourists bent on unbridled photography. Wall rage is not unheard of – some sections are very narrow.

Pick the moment right, early in the day and the walls are the walker's own domain. They provide a unique view of the city and, from the perspective of the archaeologist, a sense of scale in respect of this legionary fortress. It is not every day anyone can walk around the outline of a Roman fort over 20ft above the ground. Even if what the walker is treading on is much later in York's history, the author and walker can enjoy a bit of pretend and imagination – it adds the spark for further investigation …

As the buildings to the right that cluster up to the wall begin to thin; the Minster draws the eye. Between the wall and the Minster would have stood a series of wooden barrack buildings, some of which were still being roofed in AD 72. There is a row of tents ahead; made of leather, they were nearly as difficult to deal with as building a wooden building. Housing eight men, they probably needed sixteen very large chaps to get them upright. The Roman troops have bread ovens quite close to the wooden wall; the smell of wood smoke is in the air. The carpenters are taking a wine break and a set of dice has appeared, and there is much laughter at the losing streak of one of the men, who takes it all in good spirit, taking a sip from a once grand but much-repaired Samian bowl. The atmosphere is a relaxed one; the fighting for control of the north is not turning out to be as bad expected. Diplomacy and the internal strife within the Brigantes has been very helpful; some of the other tribes have taken the opportunity to step aside from assisting the shattered Brigantes and, as a result, York is not the front line (always a difficult spot to be) – that honour goes to

Carlisle, a long way away. Word has been received that, even there, things are better than expected – there is an air of relief. Better to be doing some serious carpentry than fighting. These hardened legionaries have seen it all and had been wondering if Eboracum was going to be a temporary base. Their opinion changed when they saw the location, ideal for a fort where two rivers meet; the gods speak where rivers meet and the omens must be favourable because the Ouse is navigable and supplies can arrive at the spot. Plus the way from the south to the fort has not one but two routes, one to Petvaria (Brough-on-Humber), one via Newton Kyme, avoiding the estuary crossing on the way to Calcaria (Tadcaster) on the road to Londinium. It feels established, even whilst the resin oozes out of the timber and the grass is making its way up through the mud, a new age is being built out of the earth.

An architectural detail in a garden – look out for more

Whilst it was very different than the fort location at Lindum (Lincoln), which had just been given the title *colonia*, there was one major thing that was the same: the land for farming – huge areas of easy-to-work land for grain, pulses and cattle. With Lindum now a centre for retired soldiers, the continuation of the Roman process of expansion allowed the soldiers to see the same opportunities and possibilities coming their way in years to come.

The carpenter looks up from his drink and sees the walker above the timbers of the fort, as if walking in the air; he takes a second look, then at the remains in his bowl and throws the rest away. His comrades laugh, the moment is gone, just as our perception of his world. Archaeology is the way of putting parts of that past back together and understanding the stories within it. It is not the great men but the ordinary, the unrecorded in text, that matter. Those that write the text are a minority; most of the Roman world didn't have the opportunity to be heard – now their past begins to shout out more clearly than the great statues and texts.

Bad booze can be blamed; the local brew is pretty primitive but supplies from the rest of the empire do make their way to this outpost – it's just a case of paying for it and building work is thirsty work. The gods have been generous, the timber has been easy to work; the local oak is good and straight, with few knots. The lads at the tilery have had a few problems because the winter floods washed through the site and quite a lot have been imported by boat.

Later in York's history there is plenty of evidence for long-distance trade and travel of the traders themselves, especially in shipping wine and other quality products. Even as early as AD 72 news would have spread to mainland Europe that a new fort had been built and, therefore, new commercial opportunities were there for the taking.

It is time for the walker to move on, but not before looking out over the walls to what were the parade and exercise yards. Horses are being trained today. The area is bordered by agricultural land; some of it is being prepared for a crop and there is a stark contrast between the agricultural and the military. However, without the military there would be no agriculture on the spot. The need to feed an army and its mounts is an important part of any campaign – a factor often overlooked. Whilst campaigns often included scavenging of the enemy's territory, this could only work for so long; continuing and improving the grain supply was always a Roman priority and the granaries within a fort were undoubtedly the most important buildings, even more so than the strong room that contained the wages.

The Roman army's diet was heavy on pulses and whatever meat or fish was available wherever the army happened to be. The time of year affected

Roman gate-site viewed from the wall, west of the present Monk Bar

the amount of red meat and the summer caused major problems for storage, so the diet changed with the seasons. Wheat and barley featured wherever the Romans went; the ability to make bread was essential, along with pulses. Could sustain itself on the march the Roman army Dry stuffs that can be readily transported and turned into potage, wild herbs and leaves in season along with olive oil and a little spice would make what otherwise would appear to be a very basic diet tolerable and, indeed, quite delicious. Field bread ovens and camp fires could be easily constructed; hare, rabbit, deer, boar and any fish that could be netted would supplement as and when the opportunity presented itself.

Establishing a new fort not only involved the physical building of a fortification but the provision of some agriculture nearby. There would have been an element of interaction with the locals through either an improvement of what was already being produced, and thus acquisition of the crop by enslaving the locals, or potentially allowing the local tribes to trade and pay tax; it would depend on circumstance, situation and all would change with time. However, the process of food production, movement and storage was as important as any other part of the Roman military machine; it is just overlooked by many.

Anything that could be harvested locally was a saving of effort and another means of gaining a better understanding of place, and by that a better control not only of the land but the people in it.

The walker should look into the fort and down on what is now the Deanery Garden and the corner walls of the fort. The walker that has managed to keep a paced-out distance from Bootham Bar to the corner and compared it from the Multangular Tower to the bar will note that the bar is not halfway; the section from the Bar to the Deanery Garden is longer. This makes the fort a playing-card shape, as were the majority of Roman forts. There are some notable exceptions, but the Roman engineers knew the system inside out and thus the exact number of trees required for the fort would be known by everyone involved; they had built these structures many times before. The one question the walker can pose for themselves is why playing-card shaped and why in the particular orientation?

The author replies that the side of the fort closest to the River Ouse is probably as close as the Roman engineers felt it was safe to go; plus there was the need to accommodate the main road going round the fort. Also there was a desire to keep a clear area between the fort and the river as a killing zone; this also seems to be the case to the south-east of the fort, where the fort stays well above the Foss and allowed for flooding on two sides of the site. Thus, the engineers allowed for as much fort as they could in the space available, which fronted the available water as either a defence or for delivery of provisions. It is notable that the Multangular Tower sits at the point where the River Ouse moves gracefully away towards the west. The Roman engineers identified the advantage of the spot.

There is no doubt that the city walls are a delightful walk. Effectively the walker is strolling along above the *Via Sagularis*, the *intervallum* road, running the complete circuit of the fort. The Minster being a constant sits immediately over the fort *principia* and *praetorium*, but at an angle to it (the church seeks an east–west line). The Roman fort takes military consideration into account, facing straight at the River Ouse crossing; however, the Minster does provide a point of site to work out the arrangements of the fort. Even the earliest of forts had the *principia* and *praetorium*, usually sited at the focal point of the fort on the crossroads of the two major fort roads, the *Via Principalis* (Main Street) and the *Via Praetoria*. The *praetorium* sits across its course and was the fort commander's quarters, and thus the headquarters of the fort; on the one side was the quartermaster's offices, *quaestorium*, and across the way was the *forum* – the offices for the fort.

The *principia* was the site of the legion's standards and strong room, normally beneath the altar where the legion would annually dedicate itself to the emperor and the gods. The *principia* was sited in such a way that a legion would parade on arrival or upon departure under the eyes of the emperor and the gods, giving them blessings accordingly.

Only twelve months before this all had been tents; a great deal has been achieved in a year and the fort, whilst a little rough around the edges, is relatively comfortable and plans would be well advanced in the provision of a bathhouse, an essential part of Roman life. A sewer system is being created, initially very simple, of wood, but this in time will become much more sophisticated. Of course, this would empty into the river, mixing with the blood from the butchers, the tanning waste and everything else, making for a fast-flowing sewer. York would have hummed in the summer months, like everywhere else did until the late nineteenth and early twentieth century; we tend to forget how clean our world is in comparison.

The walker should take note of the greenery on the outside of the wall: the trees run parallel with the wall at a short distance across the grass, which is the line of the city moat. At the point where the trees suddenly encroach towards the wall and the grass disappears is the site of the Roman gate.

The author wonders how difficult the gardeners at the back of the Minster find the patch where the *Via Pretoria* lies beneath.

The Church authorities in the early fourteenth century didn't want the traffic noise near the Minster; any gateway by the fact it is a block on free passage causes queues and commotions. So the entrance to the city was moved a short distance to the south-east, to Monks Bar, and the peace and tranquillity required to calculate the returns on the wool, general farming activities and land holdings could continue undisturbed.

Monks Bar is worth a visit, especially if the walker is pro-Richard III as it contains a thoroughly absorbing museum to this much maligned king. The walker, having enjoyed the museum, should now descend to street level; back into the present. Cross the road and go straight back up on to the wall, keeping to the Roman fort line. Then nearly immediately descend again to the Merchant Taylors' Hall, where the fort wall turns to the south-west. The Roman fort has now parted company with the present city walls.

WALK 1

The Company of Merchant Taylors' Hall

▌Merchant Taylors' Hall

www.merchant-taylors-york.org/

This means the walker has some detective work to do. Up to now it has been a delightful wander along some very physical remains with the author rambling on in his own sweet way. The advantage being that at least the walls provided some point of reference and, to a degree, the elevation physically and mentally detaches the walker from the present day, allowing an idea of the past without too much intrusion, save for dodging the odd tourist eager to fill their hard drive with innumerable images of the steps they will have slipped off through spending more time looking into a viewfinder than the actual world around them.

The plaque marking the location of the fort

Mansion House

The Roman corner tower lies immediately on the city wall at the point where the slope down from the wall meets the end of the Merchant Taylors' Hall. The remains of the Roman fort wall have been restored here. The fort line is under the properties to the right of St Andrewgate and has completely vanished from view, and will remain invisible for the rest of the adventure.

This is a wholly different image of York to that of the quiet gardens at the back of the Minster. All trace of a straight line, of any sense of a division between inside and out, has long gone; there has been expansion of York out towards the Foss ever since the Romans arrived. It was to become an area of metalworking after the Romans. The walker should proceed along to the junction with Colliergate, which is directly associated with St Andrewgate as this was the delivery road for charcoal and coal for the metalworkers. The walker should turn right and left on to Church Street and in doing so walk through the fort entrance deep below. The rough line of Petergate connects the two points; it meanders a little with the passing of time, but keeps a constancy of purpose just as it has done since AD 71.

Continue along Church Street until it meets the crossroads with Parliament Street and Feasgate. Cross the road on to Feasgate (which is not a very long street) and at about two-thirds of the way down the Roman fort had a corner tower and headed north-west. Alas, the walker cannot do so, there being a shop in the way. Feasgate enters Market Street and from there the walker should turn right on to Coney Street; the fort line is on the right buried deep beneath York. Coney Street heads up to the Mansion House and St Helen's Square. The entrance to the fort is marked on a plaque in the pavement (see p.42). Mansion House is on fine foundations, being built on part of the road. Stonegate identifies that this was the favoured route for stone delivered to the riverside quay for building the Minster. It undoubtedly was the busiest area of the early Roman fort, which explains the extraordinarily wide section of road, at nearly 21.3m.

The walker should proceed along Lendal, which will take them back to Station Road, where they started. The walk has encompassed the complete Roman fort; it has deliberately reduced the history of York to the following of a line with few references to the wider historic environment. The author hopes the blankness of the canvas is useful. The sheer scale of the fort is the primary factor that is worthy of considerable further research by the walker. This military facility could house over 10,000 personnel within 20 hectares of secure defensive works. It could be supplied with water and acted as a major hub for moving men and supplies to assist in further Roman imperial gains.

There are extremely few remains from this very earliest Roman work, save for the pottery and the burials found alongside the roads in (at that stage) small cemetery sites. The best place to find out more on the spot is the Yorkshire Museum, which is next to the Multangular Tower, where the walk of the fort wall started.

▌Yorkshire Museum
www.yorkshiremuseum.org.uk/Page/ViewCollection.aspx?CollectionId=1

The carpenters working on the barracks would continue to be busy at York. With Gnaeus Julius Agricola taking over command, the IX Legion campaigned against the Brigantes. Effectively this was a mopping-up exercise in advance of his campaign to consolidate the excellent work of Cerealis – whom Agricola's biographer and father-in-law somewhat overlooked. The more serious military activity was to be north of the Forth. York acted as an important supply base and thus prospered; traders were attracted to the possible returns.

York's Roman history is so well recorded due to the diligent good works of the York Archaeological Trust. The author urges the walker to visit and support YAT at every opportunity. There is a very good chance that YAT will be digging when the walker is investigating and that normally means the opportunity to observe York archaeology in action. Archaeology is our doorstep to the past; the walker should cross the threshold.

▌York Archaeological Trust
www.yorkarchaeology.co.uk

York is also the home of the Council for British Archaeology. This organisation is the hub for the public involvement with archaeology.

▌Council for British Archaeology
www.britarch.ac.uk

'Archaeology for All' is the CBA motto and they mean it, with considerable input to community-based archaeology projects, offering guidance and acting as a vital bridge between the professional and the community.

The author trusts that this first expedition has been a useful opening salvo. It is now time to relax and discuss the day's walk; there is no shortage of places to enjoy a good debate.

The feet may be a little sore, but the effort has been worth it. Just consider how the newly arrived legion of the IX Hispana felt arriving at a great wooden fort by a river with a few shacks along a new road, fields all around and piles of freshly cut timber feeding the carpenter's blade.

For those wishing to try the local brew, the Yorkshire Terrier is well worth a try. It comes in glasses not terracotta bowls these days.

WALK 2

A WALK ROUND THE COLONIA

- **Starting point: The Treasurer's House, York**
- **Starting time: 10 a.m. at the Treasurer's House**

After a lack of much physical remains on the first walk, with the imagination having to work overtime and in overdrive, it seems only right that the second walk should make up for this lack of physicality with some chunky 'hands–on' bits of masonry.

This is going to be a relaxing walk, just as relaxed as the wealthy residents of third-century York would have enjoyed; the daily audience, listening to claims from lesser citizens and traders hawking for service and favours is over. The work of running the colonia has not been too harsh, so a stroll to the forum is in order to meet with other citizens and glean the latest gossip.

The Minster is not on the menu for today, the starting point and first port of call is the Treasurer's House. Follow the numerous signs to get there. The author trusts you will enjoy the visit to this National Trust property, especially the trip to the cellar.

However, on the way past the Minster, which is truly the heart of York and rightly so, the walker should look for a solitary Roman focal point. The Roman column was found during works on the Minster in 1969 and erected in 1971 on its present site as a reminder of what had stood where the Minster stands today. The pillar is part of the north-east colonnade for the fort's headquarters building. Originally erected by the IX Legion, it was most

Opposite and above: The Treasurer's House

probably part of the conversion of the fort from wood to stone in AD 108 and reused again by the VI Legion 200 years later with a rebuild of the facilities. The base of this pillar was found 3m below the present ground level – just a reminder of where Roman York lies. It is also of note that the pillar came to the surface when it became imperative to hold the Minster together; the colossal mass had been relying upon its Roman remains and time and mass was about to topple the lot.

The author thinks it, on the one hand, a great survivor, but on the other, rather sad. It takes considerable imagination and an understanding of Roman military architecture to put the whole building back together in the mind, especially as it is not where it was last erected. This may appear petty and it is a grand survivor, it would just make a little more sense if it was joined by a few more and a section of roof, giving it better context and interpretation.

Across from the column is a rather attractive statue to the Emperor Constantine. The author has very fixed opinions about Constantine and his so-called conversion. The author notes for those so inclined to research further that the biography of the emperor was written by a Christian. All the author suggests is that the walker should always question the sources of so-called facts and make up their own minds.

RESEARCH FOR THE WALKER

An excellent piece of work by Paul Bidwell and Elizabeth Hartley with Simon Corcoran, 'Constantine at York': www.ni.rs/byzantium/doc/zbornik7/PDF-VII/04%20Paul%20Bidwell%20 and%20Elizabeth%20Hartley%20with%20Simon%20Corcoran.pdf.

However, this pillar does provide some further clues to Roman York in the years of full and comfortable establishment. If the Roman military in the very early years of the second century were building with such good stone, there is very good reason to consider that the rest of the colonia would follow suit. Look at the base: simple, clean lines and solid workmanship. This is solid, understated military work, replacing large oak timbers with stone ones, which will not decay. With the replacement of the wooden fort the message is very clear: the Romans are here to stay. The oak has become stone, part of the roots of the place. This announcement provides confidence and a feeling of both protection and worth which translates into even more commercial activity.

The Treasurer's House will take a good hour and a half and the guided tour of the cellar may take longer – it is worth the effort.

Having experienced quite a wonderful house, the walker may wish to consider the proposition that has been made in respect of the events in the cellar, sitting above the *Via Praetoria*, though really it is the *Via Decumana*, if dividing the fort by strictly Roman military fort terms. This would be the road that ran from behind the *praetorium* in the centre of the fort towards the north-eastern gate, bisecting the *retentura*, which tended to be the area for housing any cavalry, attendant personnel and roughly half the troops, all trying to stay

WALK 2

The Roman column

as far away from the cavalry as possible. The walker should consider smell as being a powerful influence on how settlements of all types are laid out.

This road ties up with the site of the original Roman gate, which was mentioned on the first walk. The way this road was initially discovered is perhaps one of the more unusual that the author has come across.

The author must provide a little more background, set the historic scene. The year is AD 275 and the Roman Empire has been undergoing a period of appalling instability in respect of its emperors. The legions, being a hothouse for opportunistic, profitable change, had seen the chance to enrich themselves. They knew where the power lay, not in the senate, but in the hands of military commanders that were willing to risk all and pay their troops a handsome reward for assisting their efforts. The only problem was that the legions saw different potential goals and opportunities and often these were not met; therefore they removed emperors depending on what advantage they were offered by the next willing to take the risk. Not only was there a problem at the imperial level, but parts of the empire were at risk – especially the profitable bits. Thus the Gallic Empire had seen Britannia split from Rome under a series of alternative emperors and the Roman Empire itself had been on the brink of complete fragmentation.

Fortunately, through the efforts of the Roman Emperor Aurelian (AD 270–275) the empire was tied back together, and Gaul and Britannia were back in the Roman imperial fold.

It should be noted that this imperial mess finally came to an end in 284, when Diocletian took control, but Aurelian did all the heavy work of stitching things back together.

Whatever was happening in Rome and the rest of the empire, York was back thriving again pretty quickly – it was too important to be sidelined by mere international bickering. Britannia had seen considerable upheaval in the late second century due to the uprising led by Clodius Albinus, the Roman Governor of Britain, who had made himself Emperor of Rome at York. This caused much damage to York physically as there is evidence of the withdrawal of the legion to assist Albinus (the colonia likewise was badly damaged and possibly changed its location), but the whole period of 'UDI' for Britannia was only going to have one conclusion. The Roman Empire could not afford to lose Britannia and this ultimately led to the arrival of a new Roman Emperor, Septimus Severus (having disposed of Albinus). York hosted him on a notable visit and Severus, knowing the strategic and administrative importance of the place, made York capital of the north and somewhere (we are unsure exactly where yet) he had a residence suitable for an emperor. Severus split the country into two administrative areas: Inferior, North; Superior, South; with York as the administrative centre for the north. This was the really good news York and its traders needed; the empire was coming to York and brushing away the debris of Albinus, making it ready for business and renewal.

The Roman world and in particular the world of Britannia had changed greatly since the days of the wooden forts. Cerealis fortification was renewed by Agricola, and the wooden fort lingered as late as AD 108, when it was replaced by a fine stone one; the buildings of which were extremely magnificent, certainly suitable for an emperor. A sign of the care taken in the rebuilding of the fort complex is the fact the stone was imported not from Tadcaster, the nearest spot with good limestone, but from Leeds where the stone was much harder. Elland stone, as it was described in medieval times, is still used today, known now as York stone. The Romans wanted something that would last. Even so, they rebuilt it again before eventually departing, giving a sense of just how long they were present. The timber forts would have been long forgotten; the occasional rotten timber no doubt would appear when building work was undertaken and thrown away without a thought to the effort and history associated to it – no remembrance of the carpenter and his pals and the happy hours playing dice.

The IX Legion had long gone and indeed it had vanished from most records. Hadrian had visited and moved on to inspect works along his new frontier. However, the constant factor, even allowing for the Albinus problem, was the VI Legion. It stuck to York like glue and remained in there right until the decline of the Roman Empire in the west. They may have worked on Hadrian's Wall and the Antonine frontier, and travelled afar, but they always ended up back in York.

By AD 237 York's status is recorded as *colonia*, there being no higher ranking being available in the Roman world. The rate of tax would have been considerable. Many Roman commercial centres attempted to prevent official status to keep the tax rate down; therefore York must have been extremely profitable and conspicuous for both the imperial award of status and thus the ability to pay into the State a vast amount of wealth. The honour was probably bestowed by Caracalla, Severus' son and emperor (having removed Geta his brother) who needed the money to cover the vast building costs of his projects in Rome, notably his baths. It didn't do him any good – he was assassinated while having a pee, by his bodyguard in AD 217.

The walker, now knowing the background to York's rise, should head to Stonegate, then turn right on to Low Petergate, right on to Swinegate, left into

A walk through time

Grape Lane and, when in Sampson Square, head for the Roman Bath Inn. No doubt these directions will cause the walker to lose any hope of ever finding anything ever again. Just ask for Sampson Square or the Bath House pub.

The walker will not be surprised that the walk includes a pub, but for once there is an academic reason. The name of the inn may assist the walker. In fact, the walk starts in the pub, rather than outside it. The walker should go inside, follow the sign for the Roman Bath Museum and descend into the cellar (there is a reasonable fee for the museum), which step by step takes you back to York in the third century. This small museum is worthy of a visit if only to give the walker an idea of where Roman York lies deep beneath the present city and hopefully assist in better understanding why there is so little of Roman York on the surface. Indeed, what is on the surface is the result of excavation and display, or reuse, the wall line being the best evidence and a constant feature throughout and beyond Roman rule.

Built within the south-east corner of the fort, the bathhouse must have replaced an earlier one, possibly outside the fort; Romans built bathhouses wherever they went and it is unimaginable that there was not an earlier facility. After a long day's march a warm soak and a good gossip would have been most welcome to all. The south-east side of the fort would be quite cramped for space and with the development of the quay on the Foss it may have been deemed necessary to demolish an external earlier bathhouse to make room for other buildings.

Having enjoyed the museum, the bar above serves some goodly refreshment; worthy of a moment of contemplation as to how the Romans invented *opus signinum*, the waterproof ceramic and lime mix which all bathhouses depended on – no doubt the Romans acquired it from someone else.

Administering the colonia required a corporation, not unlike the present one. The sarcophagus of one such dignitary has been found, a *Decurion* (a member of the city senate from the *curiales*, the merchant classes) buried with considerable formality.

York was a place of two parts, military and colonia, of grand buildings, commerce and power. The bathhouse was of primary importance to the Roman way of life, not only because it displayed Roman engineering and administration to make it work, but because they met a need for a social, relaxing atmosphere; getting clean was quite a long way down the list.

The walker will be aware that they are in the Roman fort, so the bathhouse visited beneath the inn is a military one – it certainly would not be the only one in the colonia.

As the bathhouse was a focal point of Roman social life and in York the rich could afford their own; the remains of water systems and baths are a relatively common archaeological find. The wealthy would have been trying to out do each other with the building of ever grander public baths (quite probably under the old railway station) and public fountains, along with a series of public structures to show off the wealth and administrative

The Roman Bath Inn

ability of the colonia. York, through its official status, had the privilege of self-government; basically the responsibilities and actions followed those of Rome and justice and government was carried out accordingly. Roman citizenship is the key factor; you cannot play a formal part in the corporate structure of York without Roman citizenship, often earned through military service, providing continuity between the Roman military presence and the colonia. More importantly, the occasional but noted residency of the emperor made being part of the elite of York a very important thing to be. Status was everything to the Roman and there was no better place to show off that status than the forum south of the river in the colonia.

However, before heading to the forum, the walker will be investigating a few other spots which hopefully will assist in better understanding how York has changed from its early days.

The walker should retrace their steps to Stonegate, merely to keep the continuation of the train of thought. The walker is an important Roman official travelling to the forum, walking the *Via Praetoria*, the continuation of the road at Treasurer's House cellar.

At the end of Stonegate, where the impressive double-arched gates of the stone fort gateway once stood, the walker should pause before turning right into Lendal. This was the spot between two worlds: the Roman military might behind and across that water the colonia – two very different places. The fort with its daily activity, its routine and formality, the protector of the State and across the way the engine room of the economy, the trading hub for Britannia Inferior. One reliant upon the other to make the machinery of the Roman world work and in very recent times that machinery had been put under increasing strain with a constant change of emperors and Britannia having been ruled by usurpers. Throughout all this York and the whole of Britannia had continued to produce goods. It was a valuable prize that no emperor (whatever their legitimacy) could afford to ignore; minerals and agriculture were top of the list for holding on to and York was in the forefront of that need to retain and enhance production at all levels. Even today York feels like a city of divisions: there is the Minster, the Shambles and old city (the tourist hub), and then there is the quite late industrialisation and urban expansion. It is merely a modern version of third-century Eboracum with the fort, colonia, marketplace and forum, and industries further out, such as tileries.

The author notes that as the walls of the fort became more impressive, the towers taller, parts of the fort and immediate periphery would have been in near-permanent shadow.

The river played a key part in York's development, but by the third century the facilities had become quite sophisticated and most of the river traffic used the purpose-built facilities on the last stretch of the Foss before it meets the Ouse. This was to allow for depth of water, the river being very much shallower than today, allowing larger craft to dock. The unloading of these vessels was enhanced by the use of cranes; such was the traffic that speed was of the essence to get the craft away and another in to take its place. There was direct trade with southern Gaul, which had been a key factor in the Gallic Empire debacle over the previous few years. Trade had been maintained; in fact, it had increased as Roman rule had been restored and all parties could concentrate on production rather than warfare.

WALK 2

Stonegate

It is also worthy of note that the quay is sited on the fort side of the river, which would allow for complete control of the collection of the all important taxes. It would not surprise the author to discover in the future that the bridge was chained to prevent craft passing above it without inspection and taxation. A similar system was in place in the middle ages.

The walker should turn right into Lendal and go across the road (Museum Street). Go straight into the park, past the Multangular Tower and across to the ruins of St Mary's abbey by means of the wide park path and out on to Marygate, past St Olaves, where the walker should turn right. Then proceed along Marygate until Galmanhoe Lane appears on the left. The walker is looking at the massive bulk of York's amphitheatre, crossing the view from right to left. The author has researched this area over a number of years, specifically studying drought marks in the grass to the right; there appears to be two very large parallel ditches (robber trenches, where the stone has been removed leaving a ditch) gently curving towards Bootham. The author is not the only archaeologist that believes the area holds a major Roman building and the discovery of skeletal remains nearby hold many clues to their likely occupation: gladiators.

The building is close to the fort and would have provided both an entertainment centre for the populace and a useful training area, especially as it would have had a semi-permanent flexible canvas cover, thus providing a gymnasium for the troops. This building would have had shops, bars and brothels nearby; the walker could enjoy a great gladiatorial show interspersed with executions, a few wines and a snack of honeyed dormouse and enjoy some exotic sexual encounter all within a few minutes' stagger. Much like any city today.

The walker should retrace their steps and at Museum Street turn left and head across the river and down on to Wellington Row.

By the third century this would be the edge of a thriving commercial centre. The major feature would be the road heading for the bridge, Tanners Row, which would have been a wide, paved way with shop fronts on either side possibly with colonnades to keep pedestrian traffic away from the military use of the road. Unlike the opposite side of the river with the fort dominating the available land, the area to the south has room to allow for expansion and, as is the norm with Roman planning, a grid plan was readily adopted, mostly to allow for the public water and sewer systems. Bathhouses would have taken vast quantities of water; a constantly flowing fountain and water supplies to the grand residences would have required considerable and well-planned engineering. The very act of getting water supplies in such quantities may well

River Ouse towards Lendal Bridge

have not relied upon the Ouse alone; wells would have assisted for general domestic usage, but not for bathhouses, even with a plentiful supply of slaves.

The walker should cross the road and proceed up Tanner Street. On the left are the outer walls of the formal market, stalls are set out in regular rows and there is covered accommodation for the fish and meat sellers. It is a busy day and the weather being good there are slaves on shopping trips and citizens mingling amongst the stalls. The slight slope of the site assists in keeping the fish and butcher's shops clean. The air is full of spices and the babble of barter and commerce is held in by the high walls.

At the junction with George Hudson Street, cross the road on to the continuation of Tanner Row (just as in walk 1); this time the scene is very

different from the shanty-like camp of AD 72. This would have been at least 21 hectares of well-organised, impressive structures concentrated between Micklegate and the present railway station. A very grand building is to the right, a massive colonnade of columns 1m wide and 2m apart suggesting a building with a first floor, quite possibly the senate building. Immediately to the walker's left are the outer walls of the forum: small groups of well-dressed citizens are listening to a legal case on the one side of the large square; other citizens are petitioning magistrates; a senate official is busy setting up a temporary notice, his slaves are busy attaching the wooden board to one of the colonnade pillars that run around the space. Painters are busy giving the emperor's statue a coat of paint outside the small temple set up to Claudius.

A little further up Tanner Row on the left is a very grand temple complex. Through the entrance a large open area in front of a temple can be seen, where priests are preparing a sacrifice to Serapis. Above the entrance is a dedication to Claudius Hieronymianus and legionary commandant, who paid for the construction. Serapis is associated with healing, so it is quite possible that Hieronymianus had been very ill indeed as this was no minor construction. The sighting of the temple was significant, next to the main road to the fort and across from the senate and next to the forum.

DEO SANCTO SERAPI TEMPLVM A SOLO FECIT CL
HIERONYMIANVS LEG LEG VI VIC
To the sacred god Serapis, Claudius Hieronymianus, Legate of the Sixth
Victorious Legion, erected this shrine from the ground

The sound of running water catches the walker's ear: there is a water fountain to assist the cleaners keeping the street clean. It is not as impressive as the one at St Mary's, Bishophill, which is a real show stopper, but it does its job.

Further up the slope on Tanners Row, before it becomes Toft Green, on the right is the entrance to a large formal building, possibly a library. Behind this and out of the walker's reach are the entrances to the bathhouse, which was perhaps the most impressive bathhouse anywhere in Britannia Inferior; it certainly was one of the biggest. The railway buildings and medieval wall cover it all and it stretched right the way through to the present railway station. There has been consideration of an imperial residence in this area, but the author thinks it somewhat unlikely if the there is a bathhouse – they were noisy places and emperors liked their privacy. There is evidence of highly decorated stonework, but there is no reason to consider this anything more than city pride displayed on its public buildings.

The walker should turn left out of Toft Green on to Micklegate. The present street pattern very roughly follows the Roman one: there are numerous shops with colonnades and a number of private residences that back on to the formal public buildings that the walker passed on the way up Toft Green. This is a street of commerce, off the main road which needed to be kept as clear as possible for military use. It is a busy spot; whilst the properties are grand, they are owned by traders and shops occupy the rooms facing the street. A cornucopia of wares was on offer; had the walker turned right towards the present Micklegate Bar the view would be just as busy, but further from the river the buildings become less impressive and more domestic; a few competing brothels and bars, reasonably close to the bathhouse, make up an entertainment quarter, but beyond them open fields. The colonia will not be enclosed until the fourth century, when the Roman Empire is under real threat and has an absolute need to protect itself – at the very moment when Britannia is at its wealthiest, no surprise there then.

The Roman street of Micklegate is below the buildings, later house builders finding it a very useful foundation; so most of Micklegate isn't really a Roman street – it covers one. The cross streets between the formal public buildings to the left on Toft Green and Tanners Row are crowded with stalls and they are not the place to linger, especially at night.

The walker should take the lane to the right, Trinity Lane. Note how it curves gently to the left. The author has speculated for some time that this lane is the back wall of a theatre; the shadow of a structure long gone. There is no doubt that a colonia would have a theatre along with major public buildings and a theatre was a sign of culture. This is speculation, but the walker can spend a little time considering this in a rather fine back-street pub situated hereabouts in St Martins Lane.

Sitting at the top row under the canvas roof looking out over the top of the theatre the walker could look straight across to the fort with its great solid bulk, ever present, detached and out of the throng. Smoke rises from bathhouse chimneys; there is a smell of roasted meat in the air; a sewer repair a block away is causing some distress to the audience when the light breeze changes direction. The actors are giving it all they are worth; the usual slapstick comedy, so popular with Roman audiences.

York is very much alive, the problems of the empire are forgotten and there is too much to do. The military authorities are very much part of the fabric of the colonia as is obvious by the grand gesture of temple building, but also through evidence of a Mithraeum. The god Mithras was just the ticket for the military, having clearly defined stages of improvement and status for the devotees. Devotion to Mithras put the devotee in the company of senior officers and promotions would obviously follow as one devotee looked after their fellow traveller into Mithraic enlightenment.

The author never ceases to be amazed with the cheek-by-jowl nature of Roman everyday life: leatherworkers, temples, snack bars, ale houses (yes, Romans drank ale), all jostling for space next to substantial houses with grand mosaics heated by hypocausts. The colours, the smells and the noise would be a shock to our grey northern European eyes.

From Trinity Lane the walker can either make their way back on to Micklegate or on to Fetter Lane. This is the beginning of a more suburban part of the city, the buildings more spread out. Some academics consider that the city suffered extreme damage during Albinus' rule and that when York recovered it spread more towards the area of the railway station, attracted by the baths and the public places erected there. It would still be jammed full of properties, but more domestic than public.

There is evidence that over the centuries the expansion of the city meant earlier Roman burial sites were destroyed and disturbed by later construction; as burials are always away from habitation and forts this gives some indication of the rate of expansion of any settlement. In the case of York burials seem to have been disturbed at the Mount, Bootham, Toft Green and Micklegate. Romans wanted to be remembered in death, the worst possible thing that could happen to a Roman was to be forgotten, so burials were usually in sight of a road where anyone could notice the departed, and family and comrades could pay passing respect on a regular basis. As the earliest burials would be along the roads to the fort, burials would have been the first to succumb to later development as the town expanded these. Most burials would only have had a wooden notice at best and that would have soon rotted away; the graves would have been forgotten. However, there were graves, previously mentioned, found at the site of the present railway station which are not on a principal road; they are very expensive stone sarcophagus burials. The Emperor Severus died in York in AD 211 and was duly cremated; the author wonders if there was a great imperial mausoleum erected to the left of Fetter Lane, one that was subsequently built all round as a need for housing in the city became acute. The site may have been vacant in AD 211 if the city had been badly damaged; it would have had a grand view of the river, was close to the fort and would explain why some academics and archaeologists think there could be an amphitheatre on the spot – it could possibly be a mausoleum not unlike that for the Devine Augustus in Rome, a circular structure of good proportion. Only a theory, but one the walker can mull over.

It has been a long day. At the bottom of Fetter Lane the walker should turn left and then right at the junction; they should head over the bridge and make their way to Walmgate. There are plenty of excellent eateries and some fine refreshment to be had. There is a reason for suggesting Walmgate – all will be revealed in Walk 3.

Find me!

Above: A late Roman multi-angular tower, with much rebuilding

Right: A rustic view

Below: Curved anomaly – possibly the remains of large gladiatorial arena

Site of the Roman cavalry barracks

The Roman gate site at Micklegate

The site of a lost castle

Descending from Baile Hill

The walkway along the city wall

Clifford's Tower

Lendal, pumping station

Bootham

King's Manor

The results of Henry VIII's handiwork

King's Manor inner court. What history this portal hath seen – and still does, as it leads to the archaeology department

Micklegate detail: statues instead of severed heads for embellishment

York Minster

Early morning in York: The Shambles

'A time to sow'. The Almshouses

Queens Staith

The Guildhall, which potentially incorporates part of a Roman bridge in its foundation

Industrial archaeology at work: a restored advert

Central Methodist Church, St Saviourgate – Roman temple or Methodist church?

The Ouse at dusk

WALK 3

ANGLIAN TIMES

- **Starting point: Walmgate**
- **Starting time: 10 a.m.**

Author's suggestion: Melton Too for a coffee, or even breakfast! He does so because Melton Too only uses local produce and promotes local food initiative and we all should be responsible in assisting local economies and reducing the distance between field and plate.

The Roman age in Britain is at an end, the only thing is, nobody quite believes it. The Roman legions are withdrawn to mainland Europe, the imperial mints are closed and a stark realisation falls upon the brow of the citizens of York: the world has just become a strange, frightening, and dangerous place.

This wasn't an overnight departure; the Ladybird books depicting legions departing with a sunset to add to the sombre mood (wearing first-century military equipment as if they had just been on a fancy-dress night out) has always been rather short of the actual mark – more a subconscious projection by the artist, for Roman read British Empire, the world changing forever, hard to accept.

The author mentions this because ends of empire are never easy, they are not clear cut. Just as the end of the British Empire was an inevitable domino effect of people, places and circumstance, acceptance (especially in Britain and in the establishment) was minimal; denial of the actual facts and continuing regardless of the consequences was the order of the day. The author is of a generation that was still being educated to run an empire that hadn't existed for ten years.

Cities and major centres of population had taken a bit of a beating from the 350s onwards: increasing problems with tribes outside the empire, mainly caused by the considerable wealth being generated in Britannia. None of this was particularly assisted by a policy of increasing the Roman military numbers by bringing in the 'barbarians' and training them – they lapped up the discipline, the methods and of course had all the skills necessary to make things very difficult for their masters.

York, because of its long-distance connections, seems to have continued to thrive; money talks and a certain amount of greasing of palms quite probably saw the less scrupulous businessmen doing private deals with those outside the crumbling empire. There would have always been trading links, so there would not be anything out of the ordinary, save for the fact raids on estates might well have been organised by locals rather than anyone from across the North Sea. This was to happen again in the ninth century, when all the blame fell on the Norse despite much of the barbarity being of a local origin due to a change in the local tax allowances of the rich. Things are never quite as black and white as they seem.

Popular perceptions of the end of the Roman Empire and the Dark Ages that follow need addressing. Firstly, they were not dark; they were full of rich colours and light. Secondly, there was a plethora of kingdoms, administration and education, which is not the chaos that the period is often viewed as. Thirdly, the idea that Britannia was brought low by invading people with helmets with horns sticking out of them is false.

It has been an unofficial bit of British propaganda dating back to the late nineteenth century to equate the fall of Roman Britain in direct relation to the rise of Germany under Bismarck. A Britain that had no empire would be weak and destroyed by the forces from without – it would be the end of everything; destruction and darkness would ensue just as it had done when the Romans left the blessed British soil. The Germans were a threat; chaos would ensue.

The kaiser was an imperialist with a passion for archaeology and the Roman army, which was even more of a threat for the British. As far as the British were concerned they were the sole inheritors of imperialism.

Britain had a classically trained academia and all of it was establishment led. It therefore basically refused to look at the documentation from the period which lay quite openly available in countries such as Denmark, Norway,

Sweden and Germany, preferring to cling to the Dark Ages theory with a bit of Arthurian myth thrown in – a very useful king that takes on all comers, especially if they happen to be foreign.

It is only in the very last part of the twentieth century that this deliberate distortion of history was slowly being revealed and it will take probably another half century for the inexactitudes to be written out. It is a disgrace that the peoples of Europe know more of the period between the fifth century and the tenth than the public in Britain.

The author has calmed down now, but it is a valuable rant because it helps to set the mind of the walker to a fascinating part of York and Britain's history. Too often York is portrayed as a Viking centre, missing out all the rest.

Imagine an old Second World War airfield, disused, deserted buildings, fences falling down, weeds everywhere, the control tower windowless, decay blooming in every nook and cranny. Once the hub of an enormously complicated killing machine with administration, a supply network, housing for personnel and associated entertainment centres, creator of a local economy – it is reduced to no more than a scar on the landscape, all systems departed without a trace, not a soul left to remember what had gone before. Multiply this by 400 or 500 sites – camps, forts, fortresses, coloniae – all decaying away through imposed neglect. Some will transform because of their location, others will physically vanish from the landscape, weeds acting as history's page turner.

The Roman Empire faded away and without a central administration and a willingness to pay for public services, the infrastructure blocked up, broke and fell down. It didn't happen overnight, so if we say that all formal Roman administration had stopped in York by 410, what world were the inhabitants living in then?

The archaeology is beginning to show a change in location, a move from the colonia south of the Ouse to that of the lands between the Ouse and the Foss closest to the quay, with the fort, in a much reduced state, still acting as a focal point, not so much for its military might but its religious one. Christianity has taken up the space left by the last commander.

This should come as no surprise: the moment the elite of Rome understood that being pope was more powerful than emperor, the empire changed in nature. In many respects the administrative channels remained strong and assisted the transformation. Whilst Rome in one respect had left it was continuing to have a very strong influence and would ultimately crush all opposition as effectively as a legion. The Christians had a powerful weapon in everlasting life and salvation which made all other religions pale in comparison.

The ruins of St Mary's abbey

York having a direct (if wet) connection to the rest of the Roman world would not vanish off the global map. Being a trading hub, it would have suffered from the climate changes affecting crops and creating high food prices and wealth for a few in Britannia, and starvation for a great deal more. Also, with the fashion for African ivory, it would have seen plague. Plague would always be a constant companion to the city because of its trading – populations would be decimated; normally they would recover, but a key factor was changing the face of York. The elite in both Inferior and Superior by the early fourth century had truly massive estates and power, and could buy off all incomers (there were plenty of them from the fringes of the empire). Inevitably, the situation became so 'hot' for the elite that eventually they seem to have moved, one by one, out of Britannia to Europe. The empire that Albinus had dreamed of eventually emerged as a few extremely wealthy families that could afford private armies to protect themselves and, of course, fight each other; the Western Roman Empire was in chaos, mostly created by infighting among the elite, with the German tribes joining the melee, raiding trading vessels and generally exploiting a commercial opportunity. Some sense would eventually emerge from all of this, but inevitably York and all of Britain suffered, the world became a very dangerous place and any major store of wheat or grain was certainly to be well protected. The public baths closed: no wood for the furnaces, nobody to clean the drains. The water supply dried up, the colonia slowly closed down; the streets were dangerous and no repairs were done. The wealthy were long gone and the roofs began to fall in. Within only a few years the colonia was no more than a crumbling wreck. Timber was 'harvested' from the ruins for firewood.

However, throughout this, trade up and down the Ouse continued, contact with the outside world was not lost; the trading was more dangerous than it had ever been, but it was this vital link that saved York from total extinction.

It was through this trade that the inevitable change in the populous took place, the vacuum created by the elite heading for sunnier climes leaving precious land for the taking. They made room for the arrival of the Anglii or Angles from what is now the Schleswig-Holstein part of Germany. This is not so much an invasion, more a case of opportunism. Vacant land which can produce a crop with good trading ports and a local population in turmoil that doesn't actually need much subduing, led more to a case of integration, and thus the Angelfolc, which mutates into the English folk in years to come, arrive.

York's physical presence is such that its Roman walls cannot be ignored; a truly monumental sight, it makes a very useful capital for the newly established kingdom of Deira under King Aelle, who called the city Eoforwic. Things don't go completely according to plan and the Deira have trouble with their neighbours to the north, the Bernicians, but by 616 King Edwin kicks the neighbours out and makes a crucial alliance with Kent by marrying Ethelburga, whom just happened to be Christian. By the end of 625, a chap by the name of Paulinus, on the private staff of Ethelburga, was named Bishop of York. Bishops need a church and a section of the *principia* of the fort would do rather nicely and a rather hastily constructed wooden shed next to the royal cemetery did the job to allow for a formal conversion ceremony of Edwin.

Edwin, having noticed that others had rather grander churches than his shed, was acutely aware that something must be done, especially as he was living in the remains of the *praetorium* and *principia*. It would be politic to provide the Church with a more appropriate new building, because such acts get reported to the pope in Rome. A tick in the box for Edwin; legitimacy in the eyes of the Church is no bad thing.

Bishops could only be appointed by the pope, so it is clear that there was still a direct communication route and Roman influence, if submerged, was still in place. Edwin dedicated his new church to St Peter, thus cementing relations with Rome.

WALK 3

Things took a turn for the worst in 631, when Cadwallon and Penda and their armies attacked, and in 633 Edwin was killed away from the city. Cadwallon took up residence and resisted all attempts to get him out, showing that York's fort walls were still capable of holding off attackers – it didn't do Cadwallon any good as around 634 (the Venerable Bede is a bit dodgy on dates) he was killed by King Oswald and relative normality returned to York, and the Minster church, not yet completed, could be continued. Wars aside, it was work as normal on the house for God, which was convenient as Oswald interred Edwin's head in the building to add to its status. Shrines were as important to Christians as other religions and inevitably they needed candles to light them; it therefore comes as no surprise that the whole Minster church went up in flames in 741.

The library seems to have survived this conflagration and York in general rises from these ashes to very splendid heights through the efforts of the greatest intellectual mind in Western Europe, Alciun. York became the place to be for learning; the fire appears to have created a stir across Europe and young intellectual minds were drawn to York both to assist and create something important to allow York to flourish in a religious and educational way.

THE AUTHOR HAS A THEORY

Under Alcuin, York became widely known as the 'Alternative Rome'; you don't get that title without something very special indeed going on. This got the author pondering. On this walk the walker will visit two ancient religious sites with eighth-century foundations and pass another, the Minster. Alciun describes it as an alternative to Rome: Rome has seven hills, which York lack; St Denys' sits on an island next to the river, St Mary's (which the walker will visit later) sits on a hill. The author wonders if there were seven impressive churches, which for the time would have been a very ostentatious and noteworthy city. Some candidates for inclusion within the seven could be St Helen's-on-the-Wall, Aldwark (demolished) which may have had an eighth-century foundation; St Helen's, Stonegate; St Martin, Coney Street.

The walker is encouraged to have a go – the rule is the foundation must be before the tenth century.

York was attracting the great and the good to its door, enlightenment amongst the disparate ever-changing world, like plonking Oxford down in the middle of the Afghan War. York was a vulnerable but revered place with international links that even the enemy had some need for communication through.

St Denys's church, Walmgate

The walker having survived the author's witterings (necessary though they are to set the scene), is probably wondering why they are on Walmgate, which is some distance from the Roman fort and on the opposite side of the river to the colonia.

Firstly, the colonia has gone, a few ruins stand above the trees and shrubs. Wood was the building material of choice for York's new building as it doesn't need long, dangerous miles on board ships or wagons; there was also no means of paying for the labour, or if there was it was far too expensive. Those buildings that are made of stone were being built out of the remains of the colonia, a relatively handy quarry.

The Roman Bridge site

The walker should proceed to the Foss bridge; this quite attractive structure is modern (1811) in the context of the Foss. The Ouse and Foss were much wider rivers than they are today, but shallower as modern sluices keep the rivers controlled. The Foss, named from the Latin *fossa*, simply means ditch, which to the author suggests possible Roman engineering in and around its connection with the Ouse.

In post-Roman times the remains of the Roman bridge can only be imagined; it would undoubtedly have been damaged and rebuilt but remained the only sound foundation for a structure crossing the Foss.

The walker should head towards St Denys' church (past Melton Too); the author trusts the walker has noted that this church sits on a mound. It does so because it sits on a great deal of history; a microcosm of York. There is evidence to suggest a Roman temple on this site, though this may be a case of Roman stone being reused; however, there are Roman burials associated with the site. The present church is worth a second look and there is much of architectural interest, so do make a contribution to keep it standing up. Note the fact that the church is effectively an island, not just because of the roads that encircle it and the distance from the Foss bridge. It may be that this was the first bit of land above the floodplain and was therefore seen as suitable for burials in Roman times and subsequent generations after in this part of the city. It does give an indication of how the river affected the shape and development of York.

The walker should continue along Walmgate to Georges Street, turn right and continue down it all the way to the junction with Paragon Street; this can be a very busy spot. Turn right on to Paragon Street, cross the road and turn left into Fishergate. Proceed along Fishergate until the junction with Fawcett Street hoves into view on the left. On the right is Blue Bridge Lane. Cross the road when safe to do so.

The walker should take in the surroundings. Not the usual tourist view of York; instead it is effectively two brick walls heading for the river. The walker should note the slope down towards the river and then remember the position of St Denys' in relationship to where on the slope it would lie – at the top. The river and its ability to flood is undeniably a factor in York's ancient history.

Archaeological excavations on Blue Bridge Lane and the nearby Fishergate House have revealed parts of Anglian York: basically, as the land was subject to flooding, the rubbish tip. Rubbish tips are extremely useful to the archaeologist as they provide all the little bits of evidence of human life that make it just that – human. All sorts of bits and bobs were discovered here – loom weights, scraps of metal and carved bone – all suggesting a craft centre of some size

WALK 3

Jorvik Viking Centre

and employing the very best craftspeople. Their customer was the king and the establishment, and they were slap bang on the right spot to receive all the precious materials, being a very short distance from the river quay; there is no coincidence in their positioning right next to the major export point and there is good reason, by examination of the animal bones found on the site, to believe that internationally acclaimed craftspeople would be in residence, with the king paying in comfortable lodgings and three square meals a day – which is more than anyone else would be getting.

The Romans, having realised this was not a suitable spot for building, had taken advantage of the river's silts and grown crops on the spot, but from about 700 to 850 the place was a thriving workshop, producing works that would have been seen throughout the known world. The evidence for metalworking and York's status as a capital meant that a mint would have lain very close to the royal palace, safely within the Roman fort walls.

Something disturbed the arrangements in the 850s; possibly a change in the security situation, raiding was not unusual (the balance between the profits of trade and the danger of attack were a personal fragile balance that the trader elected to live with), but this was different as the site seems to have been abandoned. The River Foss is possibly the clue; it seems to have suffered silting up, caused by deforestation further along its course. This may have meant that the quay may became difficult to use and the centre of trade may have shifted closer to the fort. The author theorises that if this deforestation was so intense that it affected the river, was it to supply timber to create structures and charcoal for a rising population and an increase in metalworking?

The walker should enjoy the river view – it is a very graceful spot – and then walk along the river and cross the Blue Bridge constructed to lift so as to allow craft trough to navigate the Foss. Head over the bridge and keep to the riverside walk and enjoy the stroll. Follow the excellent signage for Clifford's Tower, near to which, in Castleyard, a wonderful Anglian hanging bowl was found. Continue on to Coppergate, and follow the Jorvik signs. The walker will note that the settlement at Fishergate is a reasonable distance from the fort; it is in a vulnerable spot in the event of an attack. This suggests that it was founded in a period of stability or it had a very good look-out and communication system. It seems unlikely that a king would put his valuable craftspeople at risk unless they were so highly prized that they didn't have to fear annihilation, more a case of a change of client.

Coppergate is a big shopping centre and the site of a key archaeological excavation that unearthed a major Anglian find: one of the finest pieces of Anglian metalwork, the Coppergate Helmet. This wonderful survivor turned up after the Coppergate dig had been completed, a dig that led to the major explosion in Viking understanding and the creation of Jorvik. During the construction of the shopping centre an excavator shovel unearthed it. After all the delicate work was done a mechanical digger added enormously to our understanding of this era before the Norse turned up. The helmet can be viewed in the Yorkshire Museum. Dated from around 770, it would have been worn by a man who probably strolled around the fort and made purchases from the craftspeople on Fishergate.

Dropped into a well, possibly to hide it because it is not the sort of piece that would just be thrown away casually and not attached to a head, its survival is a clarion call for more studies into the sub-Roman-period York. The fortunate factor is that the helmet was not the only item found, nor is it out of its context; the streets hereabouts are not of Roman origin – Blake Street and Goodramgate appear to be a new Anglian town centre. Pottery finds suggest it was a place of inns and shops, all supplying the fort and palace with services, just as the Roman colonia had done all those years before. Goodramgate breaks with the traditional pattern but is evidence of development and stability and the need to avoid major (unknown) buildings within the fort boundary.

The author recommends the walker takes some refreshment in the Three Tuns Inn. It is an opportunity to reflect on the fact that yet again the past is elusive, the merest archaeological smidgen. Whilst everyone has been trundling round the tourist hotspots, until the walk reached Coppergate things were looking very thin – that's because they are.

The only standing monument to the Anglian era probably isn't, but it is worthy of investigation. So, if the walker is suitably refreshed, it is time to head from the Three Tuns to Abbey Gardens – yet again!

Turn right out of the inn, bear left at Castlegate and then right on to Clifford Street. After that turn left on to Spurriergate then on to Lendal and across the road into Abbey Gardens. Head for the Multangular Tower and just through that hole in the wall there it is the Anglian tower. It is quite possible that the walker has already seen it.

The problem is that the date is a tad unclear; it does fill a gap in the Roman wall of the fort which also shows how much had changed, been demolished, repaired, knocked down and rebuilt yet again. The major problem is the reuse of Roman material and the hurried nature of the construction – not too hurried as it had managed to survive 1,000 years and more, even if it was buried by later banking. The author is reasonably happy with the evidence, but others are still unsure, suggesting it is a very late Roman construct. Whatever is the case, it was standing in the eighth century and the Coppergate Helmet might well have been sparkling in the sunlight from the top of it with the wearer looking out across the ruins of the colonia as workers stripped stone to restore the fort. This was a process that would continue until there was nothing left but the roads and a few small wooden houses with pigs running around a remnant of the forum.

Probably an Anglian tower, though the date is open to debate

The York timeline in stone

If the walker has not been into the Yorkshire Museum, this is the time to do so and see the objects that the author has brought to your attention. Take a close look at this forgotten history and bring it alive.

The last port of call is St Mary's church in Bishophill Junior, which is across the Ouse off Micklegate, not far from the Ackhorne Inn. This is the site of the Anglian cross, a section of which is displayed in the Yorkshire Museum. The church is a remarkable survivor in its own right; the tower is a tenth-century

Goodramgate's hidden gem

structure with Roman bits thrown in. Compare this to the Anglian tower – very different in quality and construction, identifying the skills that were available. This opens up even more opportunity for debate in respect to the Anglian tower in the city walls.

▌Parish of St Mary Bishophill
http://stmary-bishophill.co.uk/3.html

The end of another day. Well done.

WALK 4

NORMAN CHANGES

- **Starting point: Clifford's Tower**
- **Starting time: 10 a.m.**

Norse York knew it was on the back foot when William the Conqueror arrived in southern Britain; indeed, it was on the back foot before that. The departure of Eric Haraldsson and the power-broker Archbishop Wulfstun had been a turning point and there had been problems ever since. The kingdom of Wessex had imposed rule on York and the whole Danelaw system, and its commerce and trade routes were coming under strain from internal competition. This was namely the Normans, who were controlling traffic across the English Channel and attempting a diplomatic coupe against the English King Harold Godwinson.

If Harald Sigurdson, King of Norway, didn't act fast William would gain the prize; so he set off with a major force across the North Sea, heading straight for York. What Harald clearly understood was that immediate action was the only way to stop the rot but his need for urgency probably led to a fundamental mistake in his military strategy; his need for speed meant his forces were spread out and the Battle of Stamford Bridge (25 September 1066) against King Harold Godwinson's army was a complete and fatal disaster.

It cannot be overemphasised that this was the end of an entire age, a last gasp. The reality was it would have changed anyway, it had already changed; the northern kingdoms were succumbing to new well-organised politically adept leaders with centralised government. The Church was providing the administration and education, and diplomats were replacing armies.

Harold Godwinson yielded to William on 14 October 1066 and Britain had a new leader, one that would make sure everyone knew who was boss. The old order was gone, but it was going to take some taking on board; the entire system – the elite, everything – was going to be trashed from day one.

York, with its communications, was fully aware of what was heading its way. Meanwhile, trading continued and there was a determination to keep contact with the Norse states – there might be a chance of restoring things if William could be kept in the south.

He couldn't. After establishing himself in London, William commenced a massive reorganisation of the way Britain was run; the elite were out on their

Barley Hall

ear, their estates given to Norman masters – wholesale root and branch. Added to this, York was a particular target for William; not only was it the base for any competitor to take control of the kingdom, but the Archbishop (Ealdred) had initially backed another contender, Edgar Ætheling, before changing his mind to William. William was rightly wary and kept Ealdred on a very short string. William was aware that Archbishops of York were power brokers and this one was never going to be out of his sight.

Jorvik became York, easier to say, especially if you happen to be speaking Norman French. Communication and thus names of places were changing throughout the country. The author considers this perhaps the most momentous change of all; change a language and the people are lost – they do not understand, they just do as they are told, especially if poked by a sword. Latin was only available to the elite, thus the Normans could proceed without the locals really being able to catch them out. This would change in time, but initially language was a useful tool for the Norman lords.

Initial Norman contact with York was hostile; the Normans were fully aware of the links it had with the Continent. Standard Norman practice was to establish a military presence and dominate the locals. This wasn't going to be easy in the case of the people of York.

Perhaps William was testing the waters with York, because whilst his troops established a base they do not seem to have chosen the obvious ex-Roman fort site, which whilst decrepit was still a viable defendable spot. William would have expected local resistance (the Norman army was facing it everywhere) and for further trouble to come up the Ouse; as it did. He placed two forts to the east of the city, one on each side of the river.

The construction of the northern motte would have meant a great number of buildings having to be destroyed, causing huge resentment and fury, especially as the residents would have been forced to destroy their own homes and work on a building that had caused their personal loss.

Both castles were overcome in the ensuing fight for York and northern Britain, but the Normans retaliated by destroy the entire city by setting it ablaze, thereby preventing anyone using it as a power base.

The author believes that William was fully aware that York would be a difficult nut to crack and his apparently relatively light initial fortification and overlooking the strategic possibilities of the Roman fort may have been a means of flushing out the contenders for the north: Edgar Ætheling, the last legitimate heir to Harold's throne, and Sweyn II of Denmark, who saw his chance as soon as his rival Harald Sigurdson had been taken out of the game by Harold.

WALK 4

Sweyn II of Denmark was a forward-looking man; he encouraged the teaching of Latin and freed his people from servitude. He saw the need to widen knowledge and the use of an international language was a way of doing so.

William was fully aware of the intentions of these two and the differences of motive.

The year 1069 was going to be a very difficult year for York; Sweyn saw that the cause was lost, perhaps because the fire which had consumed the city had damaged the Minster, and Sweyn, being a devout Christian, may have decided that it was simply against God's will to continue. He was also fully aware that the Norse systems of governance were coming to an end, but he did not give up his claim without accepting a pay-off from William for doing so.

Edgar Ætheling, without Sweyn's assistance, couldn't hold York and retired to Scotland. York was at the mercy of the Normans.

Thomas of Bayeux was elected Archbishop of York in 1070; it was to be the start of a new era. The one good thing about a fire of such scale is that it offers opportunities to start afresh. There would be difficult times ahead, especially due to the effect of William's revenge upon the north, 'the Harrying' – a scorched-earth policy destroying absolutely everything that could produce crops across the north. Starvation was a very powerful weapon, especially when assisted by a harsh winter.

York was a charred mess. The Normans were not having any more trouble from the locals; they could be employed in building much more substantial fortifications. The Church and the new residents of York could have the fort, what was left of it, and the Foss was going to come in useful – it would be dammed to form a natural defence for the castle on the north side of the Ouse (1086). The Kings Pool was to remain a formidable defence until the seventeenth century, when it too silted up.

Perhaps the York residents did fair a little better than most; the Normans needed labour and the trade routes were still important. Where there are soldiers there is a need for leatherworkers, metalworkers, masons and glassmakers, plus there was a Minster to repair from the scarring of the fire. Food would be required to maintain the army and the workers, but if the north was a scarred ruin all supplies would need to be imported. York would be back on its feet in no time.

A hiccup: The year 1074 sees Sweyn II of Denmark return.

Sweyn's motives for this attack appear to be another attempt to empty William's purse. The city was hardly back to normal, save for heavier fortifications, and so this very last flourish of a Norse battleaxe becomes a full stop. Sweyn returned home empty handed and promptly dropping off his mortal coil: the Norse age was dead.

In the fighting the Minster went up in flames, and with the repair work completely undone a new Minster was required.

A golden age was about to arrive.

The walker should proceed to view the tower. The stone structure is later, but the walker can get a good impression of how formidable a site the original Norman building was, especially as the rest of it is where the present museum stands.

The author encourages a visit to York Castle Museum; the experience will provide a better picture of the Norman castle than the author can muster here.

York Castle Museum
www.yorkcastlemuseum.org.uk/Page/Index.aspx

Having now had a thoroughly enjoyable time in the museum, the walker should proceed to Tower Street, which is just beyond Clifford's Tower on the right (aptly named), then left on to Castlegate and St Mary's is on the right. This glorious church dates back to 1020 and is a survivor of the conflagration and attacks; that is to say, some stones of the original church survived in place, though the rest was completely rebuilt on several occasions. St Mary's is now a contemporary art centre and is a must-see venue.

St Mary's Church
www.yorkstmarys.org.uk/Page/yorkstmarys.aspx

The author positively condones the contrast of present and past; it keeps the imagination alive, shape, form, texture, light and dark – all are subject to archaeological interpretation. Seeing, feeling and understanding are the essentials elements.

From St Mary's, the walker should head up Castlegate and turn right on to Coppergate, passing All Saints', Pavement, a church that would have been standing here in the eleventh century; however, what is left is fifteenth century (but a treat to the eye nonetheless with its great lantern tower). Turn left on to Parliament Street and at the end of the street turn right on to Jubbergate; turn right into Little Shambles, left into the Shambles and at the end would have been Holy Trinity church (locally known as Christ Church) roughly in front of the old Roman fort gates. This was the second most important church in York and is recorded in Domesday Book of 1086; it had major landholdings making it an extremely wealthy institution.

WALK 4

Jacob's Well

The walker should now proceed along Petergate, taking a diversion right into Hornpot Lane to view Holy Trinity, Goodramgate, established just after the Normans took over. Though nothing of their work remains it is a worthwhile diversion away from the crowds; the church is an island of calm.

The walker should retrace their steps and turn right into Petergate then proceed towards the junction with Stonegate, where another useful diversion should be taken. The walker should voyage down Stonegate and seek out 52A.

Hidden away from most of the public's gaze are the remains (substantial) of a Norman house, dated to 1180. It gives an impression of what change the Normans brought with them: gone is the timber, wattle and daub, at least for the rich.

The walker should make their way back to Petergate and head directly to the Minster. This time it's a visit to the Minster itself.

Allow at least two hours and the author recommends the entire package, including the 275 steps up the tower. The author is not noted for his slim physique and if he can manage it he is sure that the walker will too. There is no finer view from the top.

Norman house detail

█ York Minster
www.yorkminster.org/visiting/

The walker will have noticed that since leaving the castle every structure has been a church, save for 52A Stonegate; this has been deliberate. The first major structures to rise from the ashes were the churches. The Church was the administrative power house and, being controlled by the Normans, it needed to stamp a distinctive mark on York. Authority comes in many guises and the Normans were not slow off the mark to stamp theirs upon the local population, what was left of it. York was filling with masons from the Continent, importation of wine was increasing and the building boom was creating a new commercial heart for the city. The military presence and the Church needed multitudinous services, and the construction of a new Norman-style Minster was at the heart of it all.

As the walker has already had a stroll around Spen Lane, it is worthy to note that under the Normans this area became busy with metalwork production and a considerable amount of archaeological material has been discovered and recorded, assisting our better understanding of the technology and level of craftsmanship employed by the craftspeople of York at this time. This is a continuation of the pre-Norman expertise; due to York's trading status new designs and technologies were readily available. Whilst there was an ever-present threat up to the Normans, it would be safe to suggest that the Norman foundation of York allowed a stable environment for specialist trades and crafts to work from.

The walker should also consider the following York Archaeological Trust website for further reading: www.norman-world.com/angleterre/index.htm

Domesday Book identifies that by 1086 York had a population of 10,000 or thereabouts, which suggests that for all the damage done the place was booming. Indeed, it was expanding well beyond the city walls along the road towards Hull. Foodstuffs were vital and, with over 10,000 mouths to feed, agriculture began to expand to meet the demand; linear settlements starts to appear. See www.iadb.co.uk/dccook/timeline.php.

By 1086 there was not only a new Minster, but a new grand church in the shape of St Mary's abbey, a Benedictine establishment that prospered through rights to hold markets and land. The Bootham horse fair seems to have been moved further away from what could now be described as the city's gates, rather than the old Roman forts, to provide a better, more refined environment; just as Monks Bar would find itself moved. New suburbs appeared, filling the spaces left after the devastation of the 1069; Walmgate expanded around the existing church of St Denys and out through the city walls. The Foss was still a threat but the old course was now covered in willow, which could be harvested for more basic housing development.

The walker has previously seen the remains of St Mary's and also visited the Norman gates into the city; Bootham, Micklegate and Walmgate are all Norman structures with later additions. So the author, realising that a museum and a Minster are nearly but not quite enough for one day has decided on a visit to a rather forgotten part of York's Norman history.

The walker should head for Bootham Bar and turn left on to St Leonard's Crescent. Look for the number 5 bus stop, 'Orange Line 5', Strensall to Acomb, and ask for Blossom Street, the nearest stop to Micklegate. Services are very frequent and this offers the walker a different perspective on York; it will be mid to late afternoon if the walker has taken their time. York city will be busy with people going about their daily lives – the past is all around, but the needs of the present are ever pressing. It's good to be able to look at York through a glass frame, anonymously people watching, and a bus is a good a place to do it from.

WALK 4

Baile Hill

Having alighted at Blossom Street, head for Micklegate Bar and then on to the wall, heading away from the railway station (east); this is a very pleasant stretch of the outer defences which the Normans erected on top of the Roman efforts, all of which had been left derelict by the Anglians. Presently Baile Hill will hove into view, a bump on the corner of the wall. This is William's other castle and originally took up as much land as that which York Castle Museum and Clifford's Tower now occupy. The sad remains are forgotten by most but, as the walker knows, this was once the scene of a terrible battle and from its heights York could be seen burning, one age being consumed by the flames and another rising from the ashes.

Today the 'Baile' echoes to the sound of cars crossing Skeldergate Bridge and the walker should descend to join the throng for some much-needed refreshment. The author suggests the Cock & Bottle on Skeldergate or the Corner Pin on Tanner Row.

Baile Hill, a costly military folly? Certainly not. Such duplication of defences and their position suggest to the author that attack by a major force by river from the Continent was expected. Let's face it, there was a history of such attack and it would equally be a folly not to take the past into account. A strong defence was a practical answer to a historical fact.

WALK 5

A VERY PROSPEROUS CITY?

- **Starting point: Merchant Adventurers' Hall**
- **Starting time: 10 a.m.**

The year 1399 sees the end of the Norman kings; the Angevin line was brought to an ignominious execution in Pontefract Castle – exit Richard II. Henry Bolingbroke, having seized the throne by popular demand and been crowned as Henry IV, wasn't going to have Richard seen as a rallying point by his rivals.

York was a flourishing city, evidence of which is to be seen to this day: churches everywhere, many of which the walker has already visited. The Church cashed in on a profitable business called Hell: it was a case of a skint religious establishment making money out of fear of eternal damnation. Church building was a good way of not meeting the same fate as Richard II for all eternity.

There are many more religious establishments which have been lost, mostly as a result of the Reformation (by 1540) under Henry VIII which saw all the property of the Church put into his hands: a simple commercial takeover and assets-stripping exercise with a bit of rebranding. In York's case the loss of St Mary's abbey and the hospital (St Leonard's) was an extreme loss to the city as it had been, along with other Church facilities, the city's physical life-support service. The only York community groups able to fill this gap were the craft guilds that had sprung up through the city over the previous 400 years

The Merchant Adventurers' Hall – two contrasting aspects

– these bands of fellows with the health and nurture for those disadvantaged in York are the clues to the real wealth of York.

York had done very well out of the age-old problem of the border between Scotland and England. The Scots had traditionally claimed Cumbria and Northumbria, making York a very useful spot for kings and troops heading north and for negotiations. Weapon manufacture should come as no surprise as York's reputation for metalworking was well established. Ale houses – which led to more than one riot between troops and the locals – assist in painting a picture of a city very busy in varied production processes and profit making.

St Williams College

The advantage of the overhang!

There were the odd setbacks with York threatened by the Scots, but overall things were tickety-boo – particularly if you were in wool.

There are two types of guilds, one for the trade and commerce part of life and the other for the soul. The most prominent of the guilds in the twelfth century was the weavers; everyone else with a trade had joined in, vintners, butchers, porters, to name a few. Each protected their own interests against incomers and marked large demarcations between trades and regulated who could do what, when and where. They checked quality, assurance, settled wage disputes and organised training schemes.

Hence the author has started the day at the Merchant Adventurers' Hall on Fossgate. The tour is a worthwhile experience to understand the scope and ambitions of the people of York.

In the 1400s York had already established itself on a European stage and became a major pivotal player in the wool trade.

However, the 'Merchants of the Nation of England trading in the Parties of Brabant, Flanders, Holland and Zeeland' were ambitious national organisations who were determined to protect their trade in diverse bulky goods (wool being one of the most important of them). They saw the importance of York and moved in to control the trade. It takes some understanding that as long ago as the fifteenth century there was international trade organisation – there is nothing new under the sun.

York merchants didn't regain control of the wool trade until Elizabeth I, when she provided letter patent to the Society of the Merchant Adventurers of the City of York. Wool indirectly drove the rest of the trade; ships carrying wool to the continent could bring other goods back in exchange.

Enjoy the visit to the hall and allow three-quarters of an hour. There are some excellent little shops to visit as well which deserve the walker's attention, some so small more than two people in their depths can be a crowd.

When the desire for commerce has been sated the walker should turn left on to Fossgate, then turn left at the crossroads and right into the Shambles.

The author is aware that the walker has padded this street before, but it is time to consider its purpose and the practical reality for one of the city's trades has moved over the centuries. The Shambles in the fourteenth century became a centre for butchers; the trade had moved from Ketmongergate – not a great distance, but the metalworkers needed more space and pushed the butchers into the city. The walker can imagine the scene, a tad on the gory side. Therefore, metal production was more powerful at the time than butchery; meat was an expensive food item and was strictly controlled in regards to its consumption by the Church. Pushing the butchers deeper into the city

WALK 5

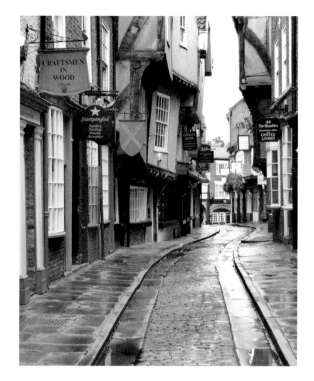

The Shambles

suggests a desire to control their trade; the need to survey their operation overrides the problems of foul smells and mess. However, one advantage is the butchers are right on top of their customer base. These butchers were paying premium rates for their land from the Church – it's clear who was making the biggest profits.

Note the houses were now three storeys high, because of lack of space; York was an incredibly busy spot and space was at a premium. Trade was encouraged by the Church to pay for further expansion of their land holdings and to make the churches more ostentatious, taking on board styles from Europe and inventing variations to meet English tastes.

At the heart of this trade generation was the Hanseatic League, a forerunner of a European Union (an oversimplification, but a reasonable parallel), an alliance of trading cities along the coast of northern Europe. It offered protection for commerce with price fixing and legal clout to back it up. The problem for York was that it was becoming a pawn in foreign traders' hands. The warnings for York should have been seen during the wars with Scotland. With the English monarch and military using York as a base, the city flourished and housing the elite led to land and commodity price rises; hence building upwards – keeping as close to the centre of power as possible. Traders do well out of extra customers generated by the Scottish wars; then suddenly with the settling of the territorial disputes York is no longer the centre of the Crown's attention. Wool, already well established, initially filled the gap, and York could survive without the presence of the Crown as long as it controlled trade in the north.

By the end of the fourteenth century York had over fifty weavers working in the city, which is an incredible number because the weaver himself would be merely the registered name and senior craftsperson; there would be an army of people, normally family and apprentices, behind the single name.

The Hanseatic League began to show signs of strain and the German states attempted to protect their own trade. There followed fisticuffs, bloodshed and finally diplomacy, but the German states gradually made trade much more difficult for York. Worse was to come.

The walker should head for Goodramgate and in particular the row of houses named 'Our Lady's Row'; dating from 1316, it wass new development for its day – a piece of commercial expediency on the part of the nearby church (Holy Trinity). Land prices being high, the churchyard was valuable, so the church had houses built on it and did well out of the rents.

As with all speculative building, they were simple in design and construction: two-storey, single-bay buildings. However, despite their cramped space, they

WALK 5

A detail from Mulberry Hall

were snapped up immediately and one tenant, finding himself too cramped, rented two.

Cramped living conditions and international trade led inevitably to an unseen and fatal visitor: plague. The Black Death and plague hit York in 1349 and in fifty years there were six outbreaks. The frequency seriously affected the birth rate and some trade began to shift to other cities. The city relied upon incoming produce from the countryside that was purged of its workforce. Those that survived could suddenly demand higher wages and better prices for their services and produce.

The Wars of the Roses, a very un-civil war between the noble houses of York and Lancaster, rather bizarrely saw York showing more sympathy to the house of Lancaster, which certainly didn't do it much good during the reign of Henry IV, who was less than impressed with their disloyalty. However, the city survived the displeasure intact, if financially strapped for cash.

There was great wealth in York, as the walker will now see if they head for Deangate and past the Minster – perhaps the grandest testimony to the medieval wealth of the city – but this is not the walker's port of call today. Continue onwards to St Michael le Belfrey, worth more than a few minutes of the walker's time. Turn left on to Petergate and then right on to Stonegate, and at the end of Stonegate turn left on to Blake Street; the walker's destination is in front of them.

St Helen's is perhaps the most notable of all the city's churches, not just as previously mentioned for its belfry, but for its testimony to the city's wealth, and expertise in one trade: the making of glass. This is the church of the York Glaziers' Guild and glass is an expensive material. York is a city that rightly likes to show off its craftsmanship and wealth. Do take time to visit the church and especially the west window and support the upkeep.

Having duly given attention to the glass, note that the skill and material needed to make it all indicate administration, long-distance trade and a depth of skill base, training and understanding which takes the breath away. How something like glass is made is a clue to our past if we consider what goes into its making.

Head for British Home Stores in Coney Street for a quick archaeological diversion; look at the glass, not quite as interesting. However, this is not why the walker is looking at a window display.

The following report by YAT gives you a clue about medieval York: www. york.gov.uk/content/45053/64848/64871/619/213339/bhsrep.pdf.

To summarise the report (one of many), York was basically growing upwards on its own filth. Amidst the wonders of costly glass production, the rubbish is piling up everywhere and being built on.

After some refreshment the walker should proceed to the river; to be precise to Lendal Bridge. The author feels that by this stage the walker does not need to be directed either to the river or to the bridge – the walker should be perfectly capable of this short expedition on their own. Go on, be brave.

The afternoon should be spent taking a boat ride on the river; it really is an essential part of the York experience. The river has played a principal part in the city's fortunes and it would be remiss not to enjoy the experience. For the adventurous there are motorboats for hire.

Take the boat trip and laze away the hours

The author trust that the walker will not only enjoy the view but take a moment to imagine Roman, Norse and medieval vessels plying the river; how much has changed and is still changing. Where once were muddy banks a fort grew up with a mighty city and then the world changed, and fields and brambles took over, then again it rose and the walls grew taller, and a great castle arose and the city pushed through the walls of the old fort, slowly pushing aside the symbols of occupation and marking the spot its own. On a sunny afternoon there is no better way than taking it easy and letting the world go by.

The river has wandered about over the millennia but of late has been taken firmly in hand. Some of these wanderings have been exacerbated by man cutting down trees and causing silting; using the river as a rubbish dump

Lendal, the chain across the river Ouse

and unofficial chemical works has also taken its toll. However, flooding is the major problem in York's history. There is an excellent website page on this subject courtesy of the York Archaeological Trust: www.yorkarchaeology. co.uk/valeofyork/flooding.htm.

Returning from the river there are two curious looking structures to visit. Immediately off the boat head for Lendal Bridge cross the road (with care) and a tower is before the walker. This is the ex-pumping station and latterly headquarters for the York Water Company; however, it also is where the chain crossed the river to prevent onward passage without payment of tolls. Across the Ouse is a squat little tower which the walker should proceed to, as Lendal Tower is private property. Barker Tower (possibly Tanners Side Tower) is the other side of the chain, which could be raised and lowered by means of a capstan, hence the circular building – the author suspects donkey power was used, judging from the size of the buildings.

The medieval era is at an end. Time for a well-earned rest, there being suitable establishments nearby. One in particular just happens to be rather handy, but that is not to suggest that other tastes cannot be accommodated – nothing wrong with a good cuppa!

WALK 6

A VERY UN-CIVIL WAR

- **Starting point: Bus stop, Rougier Street services to Monks Cross**
- **Ask for Monk Stray (Elm Park Way) or Stockton Lane**
- **Buy a return ticket**
- **Starting time: 10 a.m.**

The walker will have alighted in some slightly unexpected open countryside, perhaps better described as green space. Fortunately there are buses that pass through it on the way to Monks Cross with an excellent frequency so the walker should not be concerned that the author has decided walking off a good breakfast is the first order of the day.

The suburb of Heworth acts as a boundary to the right and a golf course lies to the left. Why has the author brought you to this relatively plain spot full of dog walkers and families enjoying the green? This was part of Heworth Moor, the only stretch that is not covered in housing. Whilst the author cannot claim that the exact spot by the bus stop is the one on which King Charles I avoided the attempts by Thomas Fairfax to deliver into his hand the petition graciously asking him not to raise troops against Parliament on 3 June 1642, it is certainly close to it, so it will have to do. History is full of places that are forgotten; it is our job to find them again.

This green swathe had over 70,000 men of Yorkshire stand upon it: landowners, squires, farmers, guild members, trade workers of all persuasions, mingling with cavalry and foot soldiers arrayed to listen to a king bent on crushing the idea of constitutional monarchy in favour of divine right – for themselves.

Not everyone in Yorkshire was pro-monarchy; however, war was avoidable if only Charles would listen to reason. Polarisation of the kingdom was not just a matter of for or against the king. England had other problems; it had begun to be truly enlightened and its people began to have a voice, a view on the whole order around them. The king was merely a focal point of discontent.

With Parliament and roughly half the nation urging for change, the Scots causing problems to the north and European neighbours creating trading difficulties, it would have been wiser to negotiate with Parliament and look at the wider picture – but no. Stubborn, irrational belief in his divine right to rule, a trait of most of the Stuart line, would prevail, with devastating results.

When Thomas Fairfax, a parliamentary man, attempted to issue a formal petition to Charles and the king deliberately avoided him (with Fairfax placing the petition on his saddle), the fate of Britain was thus sealed by a deluded king.

Charles had invited all to attend, knowing that many would side with Parliament and that Fairfax would be present; by a show of support from his own supporters Charles felt confident that he was in safe territory away from London. He was busy touring the country, making sure of a loyal citizenry and thus an army against Parliament, and in the north trying to protect his northern frontiers, thus attempting to find a joint cause against an irascible Scottish incursion. Yorkshire was divided, as was everywhere else, some on the grounds of personality of the king and others on the grounds of the desire to overthrow the whole system. This brew of disquiet was about to bubble over and Charles was doing nothing to keep the lid on.

This spot of green has no memorial but it was the site a lost opportunity to stop a bloodbath that would change Britain on a scale no previous internal strife had ever seen. It truly would never be the same again.

Fairfax had delivered his petition to Charles, which the king had refused to receive; everyone went home and a dark cloud settled over the scene – the men of Yorkshire walked home with heavy hearts. None could possibly believe how bad it would get.

Yorkshire attempted to protect itself from the coming tide, a treaty of neutrality was attempted, but individual interests saw it broken before the ink was dry.

The walker should take the bus back into York, having viewed one of the less obvious pieces of British history. If nothing else the contrast from the 1640s to the present is quite extreme; Heworth was in the countryside and as a piece of open, unproductive land was a sound place to have over 70,000 pairs of feet churn it up without great damage.

At least York's public houses would have done well out of the event, but even the author would concede that there would be a less than convivial atmosphere. The king returned to York along with his troops; not all in his company were convinced that the king was handling the impending crisis with the best of hands.

The bus will speed the walker back to reality, into Rougier Street and back to the twenty-first century. However, the walker will soon be treading through the defended city of 1644, controlled by the Royalists ...

The year 1643 sees the completion of works to strengthen Clifford's Tower; the governor and city had organised defences, rebuilt the old city walls and raised taxes for relief of the Royalist injured. General taxes were rising by the month and not everyone in York supported the efforts, not only because of the emptying of their pocket, but for an underlying support for parliament by the common man.

The walker should head for Bootham Bar, across a city that would have seen most of normal life suspended. Troops would be going about their duties; the city 'watch' would be changing shift; the ale houses would be packed; the bakers and butchers were operating normally; prices were up of course, but because of good practical planning the city was not starving. Pamphlet sellers were hawking the latest propaganda pamphlets; metalworkers were collecting sacks of scrap; and the daily noise of the city continued with an added fervour. Two years had passed since effectively York became the capital with a king and court in residence, and it had been organised chaos ever since.

Anyone with any sense realised that, with the Earl of Manchester with his 30,000 or so troops at York's gates and Cromwell's cavalry close at hand, the game would be inevitably up. The people of York had other ideas and the Parliamentarians had received several very bloody noses trying to breach the defences. York wasn't going down easily, if at all. York was keeping Parliamentary troops busy that were needed elsewhere; so the importance of the action cannot be overstated. Cromwell wasn't getting it all his own way.

The author is pretty convinced that York's citizens acted as they did in order to try and save their city and livelihoods rather than from any adherence to a Royalist cause. There were those amongst the defenders that supported the idea of a parliamentary democracy rather than the bizarre idea of the divine rights of a petty king.

The walker will have visited the Micklegate Bar Museum on earlier walks, which provides an excellent idea of the state of play: determination and no shortage of ingenuity and bravery on both sides.

The walker should proceed through Bootham Bar and turn right on to Bootham, straight down the road, past the Council for British Archaeology offices and left on to Marygate; St Olave's hoves into view. The walker should remove the present day city and consider a clearer landscape with a tower sticking out of it, providing an excellent platform for a gun with a panoramic line of fire. A series of defensive works around the building provided local defence, with munitions being stored on the city wall side of the building, out of harm's way. There were winches and cables to raise replacement cannon, ammunition and materials up the tower. There was quite probably a wall of wool sacks up the exposed sides of the tower to absorb any incoming cannon shot and, whilst relatively exposed, the ruins of the abbey provided an element of camouflage from a distance.

However, the protection didn't make much difference, St Olave's took some direct hits, as did the tower – a strategic target for any gunner. No doubt a cheer went up from the Parliamentary forces every time the gunners managed to hit it, followed by a hasty dive for cover when the Royalists picked themselves up and blasted one back.

The walker should wander through to the abbey gardens; the entrance is a very short distance down the road on the left.

The walker may require some assistance from here. Whilst the city should no longer be a stranger, the destination is All Saints', which does not appear on any modern map. The walker should head towards the castle. The city has recently surrendered to the Parliamentarian forces after the disastrous Royalist defeat at Marston Moor. The game was up; Sir Thomas Fairfax's forces are burning the buildings in the outer suburbs, partially out of sheer bloody-mindedness, partially out of a desire to cover up misdeeds and also to clear the stench of death. The attackers, the Parliamentarians, had an extremely rough time of it; unlike those within the defences, those on the outside were in a pretty bad way. The York citizens were not leaving anything for the attackers to benefit from, thus the supplies for the attackers were slim and often non-existent.

The walker should cross the road on to Lendal. The houses are being looted; the residents have run to the Minster for possible safety and smashed glass glistens in the sunlight. Arrests are being made of prominent guild members that have not had the chance or desire to escape; they are being dragged off to the Guildhall. There is a smell of burning in the air; the noise in the Shambles is blotting out the crackle of old timber and falling masonry; the Parliamentary troops are fighting each other over horse meat and the ale houses are overwhelmed with no intention of payment.

A siege that had seen Parliament pushed to the limit had been raised by activity elsewhere. The Battle of Marston Moor, the biggest mistake in the gloriously reckless career of Prince Rupert, had seen the Royalist cause abruptly brought to an end. York was cut off – it could hang on, but with Prince Rupert's cavalry gone the opportunity to break sieges and harangue the Parliamentary forces was gone. Yorkshire was lost and everyone knew it; especially the Royalist Governor of York at the time, Sir Thomas Glemham, who had only about 100 men to secure the city. Without any help the only thing he could do was to surrender with some dignity, which it has to be said he and his men were duly afforded, and they marched away towards Carlisle. Their band became smaller as they went; like the Royalist cause, it was a dwindling hope that was shortly to become a mere memory.

The 16 July 1644 was a dark day for York, but one with a bit of a silver lining: Sir Thomas Fairfax was put in charge of the city and as governor and he issued instructions to the troops not to destroy the city per se and churches were to be respected, making everything else fair game for a bit of looting.

The walker should head for Clifford's Tower. All the money extracted from the citizens in repairing the castle has come to naught and Sir Thomas Fairfax is in residence. There at least appears to be some order and discipline within the confines of the fortification, some stability as the city absorbs a ravaging mob. Under Fairfax things will soon return to some normality, but the author has some understanding if not sympathy for the actions of the attackers. They really had been put through the mill – York had not been a pushover.

On to Tower Street and across the Foss, turning into Fishergate and turn left on to Kent Street. This short street meets with Fawcett Street. Under the feet of the walker lie over 100 Parliamentary troops, not killed in battle but by disease. The Parliamentary troops were in a much worse condition than anyone could have imagined and often cut off from supplies. The Royalist cavalry were obviously very effective at disrupting Parliamentary supply trains. Whilst the siege had not been continuous, there had been Parliamentary troops around the city on and off for over two and a half years: attempts at breaching the walls had failed, starving the citizens out had failed, attempts to get across the rapidly solid King's Fishpond had failed – there had to be a presence to keep the Parliamentary pressure up at all cost. The result was under-nourished troops liable to suffer from disease, with morale low for the men having to bury their comrades.

All Saints' had gone in 1568, a victim of the Reformation or, to be precise, the diversion of the monies needed to keep it up. The outline of the building was still discernible at the time of the siege and it was, therefore, appropriate to bury the dead in consecrated ground close to where a field hospital would have been set up. The fact the bodies were stripped of all clothing suggests some attempt to stop an obvious contagion. Such thoroughness appears not to be the act of fellow troops tearing the clothes off the back of the dead, which, oft as not, leaves slivers of fabric still attached. The bodies are buried in regimental order rather than tossed into a hole. They also appear to have been buried face down; at least in the case of the bodies that the author witnessed. This may suggest that the faces were distorted by infection, potentially with dangerous pustules and thus to save the burial party the bodies were placed in this manner. Only a theory, but archaeology is full of theory, which is what drives further research to prove it wrong.

The skeletal remains were fully excavated, with ten burial pits being found. The remains are currently at Sheffield University undergoing further study. The author trusts that they will then be reinterred in a suitable location.

It should now be around lunchtime and so it is appropriate to head for a building which dates from the Civil War, the Black Swan in Peasholme Green. To reach the pub head from Fawcett Street across Paragon Street, through Fishergate Bar on to George Street, and left on to Walmgate, then on to Fossgate and turn right on to Stonebow. The Black Swan is on the right, at the heart of Peasholme Green. The Black Swan is a notable building, not just for its very friendly landlord and team, the beer and the atmosphere, but also for the folk club; the author recommends a repeat evening visit.

It is now time to head for another bar, Walmgate Bar. On the way look out that the Parliamentary troops don't stop you; they are taking grave exception to what they take to be Royalist dress. The pamphlet sellers are busy and the latest tract by one Jenkins Jones is selling well. Many of the soldiers have made themselves comfortable in the houses of those that have departed with the Royalist forces. The officers have been welcomed into several houses and the merchants are eager to point out that not everyone was backing the Royalists. Protecting York – yes; the King, well he wasn't a Yorkshireman. Fairfax's order to stop the religious maniacs from going on a demolition derby of the churches may well have had more to do with ensuring co-operation with merchants and taking an interest in their links with the Continent.

The print shops in the Shambles are busy. There is no damage here and the presses are busy with anti-Royalist propaganda and soldier preachers' religious rantings.

The walker should be quite safe as nobody is interested in Walmgate but it is a bit of a mess; the stonework has been shattered by a barrage of cannon fire. It is still a barrier and hasn't been breached – it just looks as if it could do with a bit of TLC, but this won't happen until 1648. A couple of guards are looking down from the remains of the wall; planking and rubble are cobbled together filling the gaps. The gates are intact. The iron ones have been repaired since the Scottish troops mangled them, altogether a bit of a mess, and the barbican has lost its frontage, but it is still a killing ground, a dangerous place to be if it was being defended. The Parliamentarian forces had St Nicholas' church tower a short distance outside the city walls to use for ranging their cannon, but the barbican withstood it all.

It nearly didn't, though – the Parliamentarians attempted to dig underneath it and blow it up; the attempt failed but the whole structure was left with a bit of a lean as a result of the soil missing from beneath. Looking back along Walmgate, the walker will see troops with horses and carts piling up an earth banking across the road. The bar is deemed in too perilous a state to continue in use and until repairs are made the earth banking will have to do. In the end, the Parliamentarians that had fought hard and long to get through the bar then had to carry out works to protect it.

The walker should now head to Dean's Park to the north of the Minster. Here the walker will find York Minster Library; the walker should go in, remembering first to turn off mobile phones and to follow all instructions regarding personal effects and suitably adjusting the volume of their voice.

This is a rather different afternoon; it involves reading and taking time to consider various texts that the author has selected – not necessarily all, but the walker is urged to get a feel for the times. The language is accessible and the author leaves the walker to make their own conclusions of the age.

The staff do not bite; they are friendly and extremely knowledgeable souls. There will be a preamble, but ask to view the following works. Here are the reference numbers. Try one or two at least:

000512583

000512931

000512250

000512254

000512159

WALK 6

Minster Library – treasures lie within

It is a mark of the importance of the written word that a publisher in York could readily support the Royalist cause, work throughout the siege and continue with the work of publishing without major hindrance after it. One Stephen Bulkley, did so, moving to Newcastle in 1646 and living long enough to see in the Restoration – just going to prove that publishers are basically indestructible. The author knows it all too well!

Take your time over this; feel free to ask for help and other examples, and read between and over the lines. There is much sarcasm, humour, venom and downright hatred on some of the pages. This is all our pasts – long before Twitter the word was available on every street corner; pamphlets were scurrilous, dangerous, funny and frankly mad. Much of the population was educated enough to read and those that couldn't could listen; hence in many cases the pulpit became the loudspeaker of its day. Whilst cannon and pike were smashing skulls, the real war was the word and both sides wielded it with considerable might. It is easy to stereotype the sides, king *v.* parliament, but in reality the situation was much more complicated and Cromwell's rise to power is the consummate performance of a military-minded politician and first-class tyrant. The author can never quite grasp why politicians of all parties see Cromwell as worthy of praise in respect of themselves; he would have been the first to have them permanently removed.

The walker should take advantage of the services offered by the library and there are always publications for sale.

Enough of study, there is one more call for the day.

The walker should head for Stonegate and the Old Starre Inn. The author's long-suffering editor will no doubt be tutting about him taking the walker on yet another of his pub crawls. However, he will robustly defend himself on the grounds of historical fact and pertinence to this particular adventure. Plus it has been a long and somewhat sombre day – the spirits need raising. The author will also point out at this juncture that only the liquid ones appear on his list; the ethereal type that wander York don't quench a thirst – though many, having amply imbibed, have claimed to see such ethereal forms.

The Old Starre Inn is not only the oldest licensed premises in the city, but was also the Parliamentary forces' hospital and temporary mortuary for the fallen upon taking the city.

The Old Starre can be a busy, lively spot which at every opportunity the author will (by choice) sit outside in the yard to enjoy his drink. The place is well run and has friendly staff, and the author highly recommends a visit. However, he has a slight but personal trepidation. There is something about

WALK 6

the place; the past tends to come screaming back to him when he walks in the door and so a story unfolds …

A YORK GHOST STORY?

In his life, the author has seen the result of mass human slaughter first hand with all the grim reality of flesh not attached to bone; he understands the impact upon the mind. Fear is part of us and is a great trigger that does not require a finger to switch on.

The author is not easily shaken: his archaeologist father would oft as not spend time talking to the residents of the spot he was digging, not the flesh and blood ones; no, he would merrily chat away to whomever came to ask what was going on or some that were just curious as to who he was. These characters from out of nowhere and everywhere seemed drawn to him and all were as far, as he was concerned, living beings and the author has no reason to disbelieve him – for what we claim to be real is oft as not a construct; not quite what actually is, more something that fits the bill of normality, what we would like to see, rather than the actual.

But, enough of this, back to the story.

Has the walker ever experienced standing on a railway platform or at a bus stop where there may be one or two others close by and then, suddenly, one of these strangers is gone? There is usually a perfectly sound reason: they have given up waiting and while the walker is not looking they have moved away unnoticed. This can be a bit of a shock to the system; the physical suddenly becomes the invisible. It confuses the senses only for a moment, but sometimes for longer. A growing sense of doubt can linger, a curiosity that shakes the certainty that everything follows a continuous expected path.

The author guarantees that if the walker takes their time to observe as they travel around the city this experience will occur more than once. It is as if our eye picks up something that should be just out of view; the merest chink of a missed view; not so much a shadow as the reminder for one.

The author will be practical for a moment (something he is not prone to do): the brain plays tricks and can be shocked. It absorbs information and where there are potential synergies it puts the available information into a package and hey presto an apparent reality emerges. Magnetic fields have the same effect of basically scrambling and recreating ideas and sensations into believable packages.

So what happens when the world around you stops being as it should? Things become slightly disturbing if not downright frightening.

The author has always been interested in railways and, cutting a long story short, he was assisting in removing some railway equipment on an industrial branch line in the suburbs of York. The day was typical for October: the sun was getting weak, the air full of rotting vegetation. The rails lay rusty and idle, and the cutting was quiet, save for the sound of three men unbolting fittings from a felled signal. There was occasional squeal as metal resisted, but otherwise the atmosphere was still, not another soul about.

The author was fitter then, the years had not come upon him, and when the need arose for some extra spanners he agreed to head into the cutting and beyond, up to the van parked in the lane by the bridge. Taking the canvas tool bag with him to carry the load he set off, leaving the other two to sit and wait – taking a breather from their work.

One thing railway men do not do is walk on sleepers; they are slippery, especially old worn out and rotting ones, as was the case in this instance. The cess is always safer and the progress was quick enough. The van was reached and after a rifle through a pile of spanners, the box yielded up the appropriate sizes and a loaded-down author wandered down the bank and on to the track again.

Everything was the same, but there again it wasn't; something was different since he had been to the van. There was something not right. The rails were singing, very softly, but there was something. But no, it couldn't be – a heavy lorry on the road nearby. British Rail had clipped and padlocked the line, the disposals crew had occupation, nothing should be running up the branch, or down for that matter; there were only a couple of semi-derelict wagons a good 3 miles away and they couldn't have moved of their own accord.

For a brief second the author felt as if he was being watched, as if there was someone else present; just a sensation and one that suddenly frightened him. For no good reason he felt someone close at hand. The hair on his neck and arms began to rise.

The cutting sides seemed to encroach on him as he stepped forward, as forward was the only way his brain was letting him go; he couldn't look back, there was something there, something not right. There was no bird song, all was silent, then the sound: the rails were singing loud and clear and then the unmistakable sound of a locomotive, the vibration, the regular mechanical heartbeat that goes right through you; he knew instinctively what he should do, step to the side, into the edge of the bank, lean back and wait for the loco to pass. He didn't: he ran like hell down the sleepers as fast as his feet could take him, sliding along like a mad skater. Fear had taken hold. The sound faded away and then nothing. He looked down: the rails were rusty and weed strewn; the birds sang; the grasses waved; all was as it was. A split second in one place, a split second in another, the two over lapping was enough to send a tremble through him and still that feeling of being watched.

He hurtled along the track towards his friends. They were laid back against the cutting, taking their ease. The greeting was inviting and disturbing all in one go, the sound of a friendly voice, but one berating him for taking so long over a ten-minute job. The author didn't argue, he was breathless, and they wouldn't believe him if he said anything.

Where had he been? A touch of sunstroke on a misty October day, a bad pasty?

The author looked at his watch; sure enough he had taken half an hour over a simple stroll there and back, a fifteen-minute walk if had dawdled. What had happened to him? He made a limp excuse about chatting up a passing girl and never mentioned the matter again.

In the way of things, this strange occurrence made the author think. Perhaps for a moment he was the merest echo of a shadow to somebody else's existence; perhaps nobody had seen him – there was no screaming loco whistle of warning. He had appeared and disappeared from someone else's world without being noticed, or had he? Why had he felt he was being watched? He rather wished that he had been seen, acknowledged, if only to make more sense of it.

The author, a field archaeologist in his youth (a pompous old fart of a director now – according to his wife) and having dug in some pretty odd spots in his time, has heard many a good yarn, but archaeologists, whilst having superb imaginations (it being an essential tool in the kit bag), also question their imaginations for that annoying but rather useful thing called proof, based on actual evidence. Fact rather than theory, dirt rather than words, is a pretty good way of summing up archaeology.

It is difficult to gather time and bottle it; it tends to slip away when you are not looking. So, a moment or two lost in life is nothing in the scheme of things, but the young author was wondering where he was for thirty minutes, what he saw and did, and what frightening puzzling chaos he caused to others.

So, at the end of the day, the signal fittings duly stowed for the night, three weary chaps headed for some beer and female company, if they were lucky, at the Olde Starre.

A beer or two down the neck and his friends had gravitated towards a group of nurses out on a bloke-hunting spree; by nothing other than chance and the busy nature of the pub the author became separated. While female company was great, he simply wasn't in the mood; the day's events had troubled him. He tried to put all the facts together and frankly he was failing.

'Saw you today at Melrosegate bridge.'

The voice brought the author back to his senses; he was in the presence of a very attractive redhead, but her opening line was for once of more interest than anything else. The author explained he was busy stripping signal fittings, not the best of chat up lines but he felt he had to justify himself and enquire if this stranger actually had seen something he hadn't. She really was very attractive, his mind was having difficulty concentrating on anything and a chance meeting with a girl who appeared to be trying to chat him up was shock enough without his puzzling experience. He enquired if she could remember when she'd seen him, attempting to appear casual and failing miserably. He was aware that if she had seen him there must have been a reason; why would she have noticed him, a man on an old abandoned railway line?

'Saw that old steam train, you shot off fast enough.'

The author was now reeling; so somebody else had heard and in fact seen a loco; he wasn't going mad. But he hadn't seen anything he'd just heard it. That sudden feeling of being watched, of not seeing but knowing something, someone was there – he was being watched by this redhead. Why by chance and what of the steam engine – a ghost train?

The redhead's smile, a few more of the same, and the whole matter began to drift away.

Morning came too soon and bleary eyed the author made his way to breakfast.

There was a grim silence at the table, a mixture of excess, but the author sensed something else. Especially as he had just seen a suited gentleman in the hallway of the guesthouse, heading for the door; he'd seen him before.

He was right; it was the manager from the S&T offices. It then transpired that someone had seriously mucked up: British Rail had given permission for the removal of the signalling fittings, but the date was wrong; the line wasn't clipped out of use and padlocked – better still a steam locomotive was on loan.

The author sat looking at his bacon and eggs, smiled and laughed, and all the hangover of the night before simply flew away. His colleagues, in equally drowsy mood, managed a chortle. Nobody had got hurt, it wasn't their fault – they were unaware that one of them had been closer to the engine than they could have imagined.

The loco had been kept at Dunnington for a couple of weeks before use and, as the section of line wasn't in general use, the crew had taken advantage of it to check the loco over and had used the bridge as the end point for their adventure. So the girl had seen the loco from the other side of the road; she, understandably, had expected it to run under the bridge in a few moments, so crossed to see it; instead, all she saw was the author running along the track. The loco never went any further towards the bridge and ran back towards Dunnington, oblivious of the S&T engineer running for his life in the opposite direction.

As for the rest, was it pure chance that the redhead found the author? Leave that to female intuition and the fact her auntie ran the B&B and knew exactly which pub the lads were using.

As for lost time, the author's watch was on the blink. He was the last down for breakfast.

That is how it is with a good ghost story; there is an explanation, you just have to go look for it.

The author recommends the walker finds a dark corner in the Olde Starre and try a story of their own. There is a good chance you will end up feeling as if you are being watched. The Olde Starre Inn is a very mixed up building. The cellars date back to the tenth century and quite possibly what are called cellars are in fact the remains of a stone-built building of some note that was on the surface at the time of construction. From a Civil War perspective the building would have looked very different than today, with a wide external yard. There are claims in respect of which troops were treated here; the answer seems to have been both Royalist and Parliamentarian. Practical field surgery may appear brutal to the eye, but during the Civil War new techniques were developed for removing bullets, sealing wounds and dealing with broken bones. The surgery was getting better, but the hygiene, or lack of it, was the major problem and still the biggest killer.

Considering its brief use as a field hospital and the deaths associated with it, it is a calm place. As a building it would have seen much before the seventeenth century and has seen much change since. It has a history, but so has everything around it. Is it haunted? No less than anywhere else in York.

The Royalist troops departed York, but the price of victory for the Parliamentarians was a steep price to pay. Months would pass before any true stability could be claimed. The Minster was given to the city, the establishment having been thrown out; the building described as a preaching house. The city and the troops needed some solace and the number of churches seemed to absorb the more manic revolutionary preachers. Fairfax knew what he was doing when he prevented the churches from being destroyed – he was allowing the steam to be taken out of the loud, bizarre and frankly potty.

> The English Civil War, or to be precise the three civil wars between King and basically everyone else seems to have more complete nutters to the square inch than you could shake a stick at and Cromwell saw the chance to take control by sharp political manoeuvring against those of sound mind seeking an equality of the nation.

There. That sums up revolutionary thought in the age of change rather more succinctly than most first-year university students can.

As for York and its citizens, there is a curate's egg of an ending – good in parts. Between 1649 and 1660, when the Commonwealth collapsed and the monarchy was restored, the city had picked itself up and the guild records show all the activity of the city functioning as if nothing had happened. Save for a drop in numbers, all the basic services of a city had been restored. The attitude must have been that York had seen it all before – it could absorb destruction, brush it away and start again. Unfortunately, the Civil War and the Commonwealth saw York heading into decline in influence and thus power. Commerce was heading elsewhere; a new age was slowly dawning and York wasn't part of it.

The capital of the north was now spent. York, like the forgotten men of Kent Street, was an echo on the wind. It remained a local focal point for agriculture and domestic trade but not a political one. York was lost in a shift towards new industry; just as wool had moved away to the east, now the age of coal and industry were to drag trade further north and east. Cannon manufacture had provided engineers with castings and designs for cylinders. Pumps and the very early sparks of steam power were being made and York wasn't part of that surge ahead. It was stuck in the slow lane.

WALK 7

GEORGIAN FROLICS

- **Starting point: The Assembly Rooms, Blake Street**
- **Starting time: 9.30 a.m.**

The coming of the Hanoverian kings saw the lot of York improve. The bickering across the North Sea had long caused trade in York to suffer. Wool and weaving had moved away long ago and the city had been reduced in importance to that of an agricultural centre with good river transport links. A key visual factor of how things had stagnated can be seen in the fact that key trade buildings are frozen in time: the Merchant Adventurers' Hall and the Merchant Taylors' Hall don't carry signs of great modernisation. There was no spare cash to bring them up to date with the latest architectural fashion.

From the end of the Commonwealth in 1660 to 1714–15, with the arrival of George I, no obvious great architectural change took place in the city, save (it must be said with some style) for Cumberland House on Kings Staith. The first sparks of the Industrial Revolution pass York by; agricultural developments slowly improved land management, but the desire to show outward splendour was balanced by a need to maintain what was already present, rather than a desire to spend on new builds. One exception was St Crux, which was built in 1697 with a tower of an unusual Italianate design; it would have made an interesting contrast on the Shambles today – but the Victorians took a pickaxe to it!

The Assembly Rooms of 1732 were designed by Richard Boyle, 3rd Earl of Burlington, a Whig by politics, pro-Hanoverian and a pretty good architect.

A window of the Merchant Adventurers' Hall

The architecture and the politics are of note: Boyle led the pro-British school of architecture (even if it originated in the work of Andrea Palladio, an Italian architect of the sixteenth century). A neo-Palladian styling and balance of composition was a mark of the Whigs – an outward statement of the political direction of the establishment that would support this new age, new king and new commercial opportunities.

A new king, a constitutional monarch, suited this age of a well-travelled and relatively well-educated aristocratic elite whom could afford to be liberal in their view of reasonable freedom of expression, including religion. The Assembly Rooms are an expression of this desire for openness; a place for the dances, gaming and political intrigue, making it a hub for York and for the growing northern elite. This was a meeting of architecture and minds all with a specific purpose.

The Assembly Rooms offered the Whigs a public platform ('public' in the sense of the affluent who had influence and could vote) to push out the Tories with their instinctive desire to protect the Church of England (whilst at the same time holding some passion to restore the Catholic Stuart line to the throne) and promotion of the rights of the untitled genteel nobility. Complicated sorts, the Tories. The Whigs had the money to rise above such things: a classical design to life, a free attitude to trade and religion (as long as it was not facing towards Rome) under a constitution, with a king that respected the rights of the citizens. The Tories wanted to rule the country and impose things; the Whigs actually owned most of it and had no intention to allow such nonsense. As a child the author can remember his elderly aristocratic relatives muttering about the 'middling gentry' – attitudes die hard in the north.

The Assembly Rooms hit the mark. They were a great success in attracting a new sense of public pride that had been slipping a tad over the last century; ever since the Restoration York had trundled, rather than raced, along.

The year 1715 had seen York as the 'clink' for rebels, mopped up and prepared for dispatch for supporting the Jacobite cause for the English and Scottish throne. This was the result of James III's only and utterly futile attempt at getting a throne that was, as far as the people of Britain had decided, would never be claimed by a Stuart again. York merely acted as a handy prison some distance from the Scottish border where some relief for the traitors might be sought. This is significant in the fact that York could be seen as a sensible spot to promote anti-Jacobite feeling and herald in the new age of Hanoverian monarchy – polite political society would replace the Council of the North and be quite effective in establishing a solid social bulwark to prevent any feelings of rebellion.

WALK 7

This proved to be a sensible move, as the 1745 Jacobite uprising by the Stuart pretender Bonnie Prince Charlie hurtled, lemming-like, south from Scotland. York was able to silence any murmuring of Jacobite support, with the archbishop and the lord mayor rallying the city into fervours of activity to protect the status quo.

York Castle again saw the Jacobites duly housed and then dispatched after the whole attempt collapsed, doing no end of good for the Scottish tourist industry and shortbread manufacturers for centuries to come.

Georgian York looks decidedly different from its predecessor. Ancient, bent, wooden structures were pulled down or hidden behind grand classical frontages. Brick was the major change; whilst York has seen brick used from the fifteenth century, it had been an expensive commodity imported from mainland Europe as a ballast cargo. Slowly it became apparent to anyone that with good clay and no shortage of straw it was possible to make brick for themselves, but there is evidence that the guilds in York and elsewhere could see a threat from its use as it reduced the need for wood and stone. Fortunately, with the beginnings of the British Empire and the gradual expansion of the pink areas of the globe indicating Britain's imperial advance, timber and carpentry thrived in shipbuilding; timber was an important commodity for merchant ships and the navy protected them. Stone masons could be employed on the grand buildings that could be afforded because of the trade; brick made the ideal product for filling the gap: the age of the bricklayer was truly born. Stone was used more for external show than actually holding the roof up.

From the Assembly Rooms in Blake Street, the walker should head for St Helen's Square and the Mansion House – the work of John Carr, an architect and a very good one too. Clean lines, dignified and always with a sense of establishment, Carr's buildings are deeply planted yet for all their show they are roast beef and Yorkshire pudding – a good filling practical dish on a very grand platter. The edges are good and the interior is sensibly fulfilling and tastefully useful.

The walker should take at least an hour with this building, not only because John Carr designed it and indeed lived in it as lord mayor, but because the Mansion House is the centre of much of York's public history. York may have been passed by – the Industrial Revolution was taking place elsewhere – but the profits from it and the agricultural trade to feed the new age were making York a hub for the landowners, nobility and chancers alike.

▌Mansion House
▌www.mansionhouseyork.co.uk

The walker, having been to York Castle in earlier adventures, will have already seen Carr's Female Prison and passed the Assizes Courts, two very credible pieces of work with much to say about changing attitudes towards public buildings and the administration of justice. Sited on a castle which had been imposed on the city, eventually swept away by a classical age; it has to be said that the Victorians then put a truly ghastly monstrosity of a prison in its place, which imposed itself on all within its shadow. Fortunately the demolition ball took out the Victorian era very neatly indeed. Carr would have been thoroughly delighted with the wreckers' work.

Away from the Mansion House the walker should head for Castlegate and Fairfax House. Carr didn't actually build this house; however, he did remodel it and the author has brought the walker here to look at the interior. Carr didn't just do exteriors; his workmen were of the highest quality and the attention to detail is truly impressive. The walker should likewise take their time in taking the house in. Likewise the house opposite is a pure Carr structure and the two are a true testament to his abilities.

York is very lucky to have the York Civic Trust; its work has helped preserve the city's past and the author urges the walker to make a generous donation to their efforts.

York Civic Trust
www.yorkcivictrust.co.uk

Their motto is 'preserving the past – shaping tomorrow', one that the author heartily believes in.

It should be time for a luncheon, or at least the author is ready for a quenching draught of something hoppy; so the walker may wish to join him in the Three Tuns on Coppergate.

There are some extremely grand buildings in York, the Mansion House, the Assembly Rooms, Fairfax House, and the walker will pass others worthy of a second glance. However, the walker should be very aware that not every one of York's citizens lived in such luxurious surroundings. The streets of York were still largely as they had been laid out during the Norse era. The building plots hadn't changed at all and the poor were still scratching themselves an existence, the only relief being the opportunity to be shipped off to one of Britain's new colonies courtesy of stealing a loaf of bread.

Over luncheon, the walker the can reflect on the great divide: the architecture of the age, Carr's substantial, classic, well proportioned and calm versus the erratic bent beams and wandering roof lines of the Three Tuns.

On the way to St Olafs

This contrast is a physical portrayal of the eighteenth century: an apparent sense of control, straight and true, versus the decrepit and ill used. The grand and comfortable actually hides near-constant strife; if not fighting the French or Spanish (not forgetting the Dutch) and losing America, the British were quite capable of the odd punch up at home. The Stuarts' attempt to regain the throne had left a nasty taste in the mouth of some and the Gordon Riots over the repeal of the Papist Act 1778 (allowing a certain amount of freedom to Catholics) led to Lord Gordon's attempt to have the act repealed in 1780 – not out of a great personal anti-Catholic fervour, but as a means of using public sentiment to fuel his political ambition. Gordon could fuel religious and absolutist monarchy fears because the masses felt completely detached from the whole mechanism of government; only the property classes had any vote at all. The result was a gin-sodden bloodbath in London, which Gordon ultimately got away with. The mob took the bullets. It was ever thus.

The Archbishop of York, William Markham, was up to his neck in the political meddling that led to the Gordon Riots. but he departed London in great haste when the rioters were close at hand. Bishops and archbishops were extremely powerful individuals with political clout. The Church of England had grown rich and rotund, and Archbishop Markham typified the politically-active clergy eager to protect their interests in a world where the churches were falling down yet the tithe taxes just added to the citizens' burden.

St Olafs

Almshouse, Bootham, otherwise known as the 'Old Maid's House'

Judge's Lodgings

WALK 7

The Church had its interests to protect. Looking with horror at the state of France and the turmoil of revolution which would see them ousted should such ideas of liberty and fraternity spread here, plus the loss of the Americas and political battling at home, it all made for a very interesting life for the men of the cloth. Whilst the Church no longer has quite the wealth it once did, the archbishops of York are still willing to enjoy the brickbats of political life and certainly enjoy having a go – whatever the subject and opportunity may be.

The author having spoilt lunch feels it only right to make amends as quickly as possible.

The walker is given a good circuitous but enjoyable ramble to find the following residences.

Wandesford House, Bootham. Originally known as the 'Old Maids' House'. It would be unfair to suggest that no one cared for the eighteenth-century poor and this almshouse of 1741 is testimony to Mary Wandesford, who decided to assist women not as lucky as herself.

The Judge's Lodging, in Lenda, is the first stop; the walker will have passed this way many times but take the opportunity to take in this 1720 build and then head across the river to Micklegate and head up the hill and look at the slightly later houses; in particular Micklegate House dating from 1752. Then head on through Micklegate Bar to the Bar Convent on the left, which was actually started in the late seventeenth century and substantially remodelled with a new frontage in the 1760s.

The Bar Convent is this afternoon's visit; it is a worthy one.

█ Bar Convent
www.bar-convent.org.uk

The walker should now turn back through the Bar and wander down Micklegate and take in the aspect from the opposite direction. From a Georgian perspective this southern side of the river provided a sense of space compared with the cramped centre. Take a close look at number 86; it is not the grandest, though it is kept in excellent condition; but it typifies all that the prosperous landowning classes could afford 'in town'. Note the sturdy front door and the shutters; the house can be shut up tight at night – a small fortress against the night and all within it.

The author muses that it comes as no surprise that York saw considerable felonious activity in the eighteenth century. There was also a fear of insurrection, as the playground of the north could be the bubbling pot of revolution. A cavalry barracks was established on the Fulford Road in 1720, rebuilt in 1795, notable as these building campaigns parallel British rumblings.

The walker, having taken in Micklegate, should head towards the Minster. Be there before 5.15 p.m. (3.50 p.m. on Sundays) to attend evensong – all are welcome. As you are attending a service there is no entrance fee. Be the walker of a religion or none, the experience provides a contemplative moment in a great powerhouse of the eighteenth century. It is very special, more so if you take part – it is the only way to understand place and how it can be used. The Minster is an engine house with many complex parts, some obscure, but all part of a greater whole. It has been a power base more formidable than any fortress and it still works. The Georgian bishops were only a mere blink of an eye in its gaze; it has seen better and worse, but they all seem to have been quite overtly political animals in a political age.

Take Archbishop William Dawes. If you concentrate hard and pop the muffled hum of visitors into a distant cupboard of the mind, you may come across his fine-toned rounded voice (which matched the girth) laying down the establishment line of 'everyone knowing their place'. Dawes and his dire ilk managed to keep the Church of England distant from the people, with the result that the masses turned elsewhere, to Methodism and the like. Christianity in England evolved in the late eighteenth and nineteenth century in direct opposite proportion to the desire of the establishment to hold the party line. No wonder acts of vandalism and destruction took place, the extreme leading to a counter extreme.

The walker should note that much above their head, although of an apparent age before the eighteenth century, is in fact the result of rebuilding after the 1829 fire. John Martin's actions mimic a populous feeling of retribution upon an age where the Church had supported a State attempting to keep the lid on the people's desire for a say in how they were ruled.

On that note, the author, suitably soulfully refreshed, will head for the Minster Inn on Marygate; he suggests the walker joins him.

WALK 7

WALK 8

THE RAILWAY AGE

- **Starting point: National Railway Museum, Leeman Road, York, YO26 4XJ**
- **Starting time: 10 a.m.**
- **Also, if planned in advance, there is an opportunity to visit the Derwent Valley Railway, www.dvlr.org.uk**

The author has been involved in railways as long as he has been involved in archaeology; if he wasn't digging up the past then he was using his school ruler to scrape centimetre-thick grime from locos at the end of steam on the southern region. Education then got in the way and after a break of a few years he was able to pursue archaeology, railways, beer and women in equal measure. To this day he is still involved in preservation, being a minor officer of the Heritage Railway Association and helping the expanding network of independent operators in the UK, Europe and beyond.

A visit to the National Railway Museum is a must and should take two hours at the very least. The author is quite sure the walker can follow the signs to the museum, which was once the North Eastern Railway, latterly British Railways', north-east region engine shed for York. Even if the walker is not interested in steam engines there is more to railways than just engines; it is social history and a history that has shaped all our lives. Railways are the backbone of the country, albeit in their withered form after the Beeching axe.

York was a major player in the birth of the national network. Not for the first time it just had the luck to be in the right place. York was a city to aim at on the engineers' map. Whichever way round they looked at it, York was an ideal site for a line from London or from Scotland. In a time when the traveller would think in days for even relatively short distances by stagecoach – York was four days from London – doing it in a day would seem marvellous. Of course, the prospect of reaching Edinburgh was a little way off, but it wouldn't be long and York in turn became a staging point in the 'Race for the North'. To find out more – the National Railway Museum tells the story.

Railways are industrial archaeology and the author has from time to time been requested to assist railway operators in respect to historical remains. In many cases these are still in use to this day; archaeology is not always a case of digging things up. Oft as not the author is astounded by the craftsmanship and vision of the railway age, and the sheer audacity of scale. Oft as not these works are hidden from public view, but no less magnificently built and finished. They showed pride – something that is sadly lacking in this modern railway age, full of accountants cutting costs and improving things by stopping them, like dining on trains and even seats.

Having thoroughly soaked up the essence of the day, the walker should follow the footpath to York station; it is well signposted and takes the walker effectively to the back door or furthest platforms from the station's entrance. This is good news because the walker gets the whole atmosphere of this wonderful structure. It should be noted that this access would not have been possible if the railway companies that currently operate the country's national network had been allowed to get their way and fit barriers across the entrances to protect their profiteering interests.

The station curve is significant, it identifies the mainline has to both head for and also avoid York. Unlike Newcastle-upon-Tyne, the railway does not go through the city's castle, but it did originally plough through York's city wall; more anon.

Do take the time to get the atmosphere of York station: it is busy, a tad faded and much of the station structure no longer has any railway purpose, being converted to retail premises. Fortunately the building, dating from 1877, was restored after the Luftwaffe paid it a call in the Second World War and severely damaged by bombing.

The walker should proceed out of the station entrance and turn right along the pavement; Station Road turns into Queens Street and the Railway Institute is the most noticeable structure (at the time of writing this area is a building site) roughly to the east side of the very first station at York and originally

The site of the Roman road, heading into the fort

the station pub. The site was cleared and an 'improving establishment' for the railway men without beer was constructed. This very first station was wooden, always a temporary structure as the railway age was ever heading onwards. The 1840s were seeing a sudden and much-needed revival in York's fortunes. Years of mouldering decline and loss of status could be reversed. The railway could restore York's prospects and direct contact with the capital at speed and in comfort was the thing. York's unofficial preserved status began to attract an early but influential number of tourists; the rich, the academic and the curious began to use the railways, and York was a specifically interesting specimen.

The walker should now proceed through Micklegate, being aware of where it is through earlier adventures, and take to the city walls, to end up standing above Toft Green. The walker will be aware that they are on a bridge, the city wall accommodating the route of the railway lines to the second station, which the walker has investigated reasonably fully on two previous walks, and there is some considerable significance in this. The first walk brought soldiers up a new Roman road towards a fort across the river. This then, in the blink of an imperial eye, became a Roman road through a colonia; then a road through a ruin, followed by a rapidly expanding medieval settlement, and now a railway is following the very same path. It makes the author consider that this otherwise rather forgotten corner of York is more important than most give it credit for.

The old terminus railway station (1842), which created considerable operational difficulties, was designed by Thomas Carby, who took the opportunity to reuse the design of the then London Euston station – Carby worked for George Stephenson so it made good financial sense to use the drawings again, especially as railway building design was still in its infancy and it was wise to use something that worked. Built as the terminus of the York to Leeds service (York & North Midland Railway) and the Darlington (Great North of England Railway) with a direct connection to London, it made it the major junction in the east of England. The directors of all the companies understood the fact that York was going to be a honeypot – they weren't wrong!

From the walls the walker can gaze across a multitude of more modern roofs, making it complicated, but not impossible, to work out the site of the sidings and where the station roof would have been. There is a very short part of it still in place. After the new station was opened the site remained in railway ownership until very recently. At the time of writing York City Council are about to take up residence, thus ending a very long period of railway ownership. The site, as the walker knows from previous visits, has a rather good foundation, more than likely a large public bathhouse – thus the site seems to keep a public persona.

The walker should descend the walls and head across Lendal Bridge, built to assist the traffic to the railway station, and head for the De Grey Rooms and exhibition centre on the right-hand side of the road across from the art gallery and Exhibition Square. The walker will have noted this rather grand but understated building sweeps around to Bootham. The De Grey Rooms played a significant part in York's railway age: George Hudson spun an enticing web here and did, to his credit, build railways and get the relatively new technology into the public domain, offering shares that anyone with a few savings could afford – not just coalmine owners, but manufacturers and the elite. Unfortunately, Hudson over-iced the cake and George Leeman (chairman of the North Eastern Railway, whose headquarters the walker will have noticed on the right at the crowded junction between Station Road, Rougier Street and Museum Street) brought him spectacularly down with a year spent in York Castle Prison (1865–66) for debt as a result of admissions for corruption.

The walker has a choice at this point. If it is an operating day at the Derwent Valley Railway the walker may like to take a taxi out to Murton Park and enjoy a ride on the railway and support a very active preservation project. The Derwent Valley Railway operates at the Yorkshire Museum of Farming, Murton Lane, Murton. The author would like to offer a bus service, but there isn't a very frequent one. To keep costs down the author suggests taking the bus one way, so here is the link to the most recent timetable. Check with the operator before travelling.

East Yorkshire Service 747
www.eyms.co.uk/content/busservices/searchtimetable.aspx?intservice=94 &intdeparting=416

Alternatively, the walker could just go for the walk on any day and the effort is worth it because the coming of the railway age brought enormous change to York; namely the opportunity to take local agricultural products, refine them, mix them with materials arriving by rail from throughout the empire, and make chocolate on a scale never previously imagined.

Chocolate, for over 260 years, was a big part of York's life: from the eighteenth-century drink to the Kit Kat, York has been a centre for chocolate production. The world has moved on – it is a sad fact that only one, now international, company remains.

The walker should head from Bootham all the way to Fossgate, on to Walmgate and turn left into Navigation Road; cross Foss Island Road by the pedestrian crossing, past Morrisons, and on to the cycle way. Those wishing to walk to Murton Park and the Derwent Valley Railway should follow this well-signposted route. The walker is now on the track bed of the railway. Those walking back from Murton Park can either leave the railway here or continue on to the Nestlé factory and the site of the junction. Likewise, walkers wishing just to enjoy a brief stroll along this ex-railway should turn left along the cycle track.

The author, if nothing else, offers plenty of choice.

Murton Park is the home of the Yorkshire Farming Museum and also has an excellent educational centre for schools.

Murton Park
www.murtonpark.co.uk

The author will turn left along the cycle path and pretend he is on the footplate of a diesel locomotive heading towards the Nestlé factory, an experience he once actually enjoyed many years ago. The track bed is very changed today and in many respects is busier than it probably ever was – save during the second world war, when it was useful as a diversionary route. The Derwent Valley Railway was a very speculative venture that if built now would have had a flourishing commuter service for those living and working around York; what was agricultural land along its route is now a commuter belt. The agricultural benefit was supplying the chocolate factories with sugar beet, which would be better than lorries. The line was never part of the nationalised network and the stub end of the line even saw steam passenger services at weekends for a while, earning the company some much-needed cash. All gone and opportunities lost. At least the track bed is still of use and the bridge across the Foss brings the walker into the Nestlés factory site and under the Wigginton Road, then up on top of the bridge. A very different part of York from the Shambles, but no less important in the history of the city. Nestlés, now Nestlé, once ran passenger services; think how many cars a major manufacturer could take off the roads of Britain if they did the same. All now lost in the moiré of progress.

The walker should proceed down the Wigginton Road towards York Hospital and the bus stop. Take the number 6 service into the city.

Bus Route Map
www.firstgroup.com/ukbus/york/assets/pdfs/maps/york_city_centre_
map.pdf

For those making their way back from Murton Park there are bus options from
Osbaldwick, which is in easy distance of Murton Park and well signposted.
The bus service 6 will take the walker back into the city.

Alight at Station Road and head for the Maltings to end your day. The author
trusts the walker will have noticed the contrast: the National Railway Museum,
York station, even the Old Station, versus the virtually forgotten Derwent
Valley line. Well done those volunteers that are keeping its memory alive. What
a short-sighted mistake to allow building on its track bed – rail and tramways
are the way ahead. Rail will rise from the ashes – it is the only way forward –
but the walker would expect the author to say that.

Well done, a very different day indeed, but the author hopes an enjoyable
one. As a treat, some refreshment might be a good idea, so the author
recommends the Blue Bell Inn, Fossgate. Cheers!

WALK 8

WALK 9

VERGELTUNGSANGRIFFE

- **Starting point: The Guildhall**
- **Starting time: 8 a.m.**
- **Pack a snack, it's a long day**

The legacy of the Hanseatic League was to cause the most dangerous moment in the history of York. In its past York had been burnt and destroyed a number of times, but the threat of 28–29 March 1942 was undoubtedly the worst.

Bombs were not dropping on York those two nights in March, it was the RAF bombing Lubeck, a noble ancient city much like York, with a grand cathedral and a merchants' quarter all containing fine works of art. Lubeck could be viewed as a strategic military target as it is a port, but there is a distinct and chilling aspect to this attack. The British War Cabinet had decided to issue orders to batter German civilian morale. Thus Lubeck, an old, small, wooden city minding its own business with very few defences, was brutally bombed in full moonlight.

Why the British war Cabinet decided this course is not as straightforward as it may seem. The Germans had used *blitzkrieg* across Europe and terrorised the population accordingly. London has been severely bombed, central Coventry had been virtually obliterated, but the one factor that was fully recorded and available to the British war Cabinet was the fact that the population although initially very shaken, actually restored itself quickly and crucially became more resolute. The British realised that; bombing the German civilian population would be no different in the result – stern resistance and closer adherence to the Nazi regime, being seen as protectors of the German *Volk*.

In retaliation for the Lubeck raid, the Luftwaffe was given the unenviable task by the German High Command to bomb historic cities in Britain. One can imagine that pilots and crews were less than impressed; risking one's life on strategic missions was one thing, risking it for the sake of propaganda was another – especially as the distances were great and there was plenty of opportunity for the British to knock them out of the sky on the way.

York was bombed as part of the so-called Baedeker raids, the Germans using the Baedeker excellent (if a tad solid) guidebook to English cities as a guide to which to hit in retaliation for Lubeck.

Exeter, Norwich and Bath had already been hit and all parties were aware what was going to be arriving on York's doorstep, so plans were well advanced to act as quickly as possible to save the city centre from total destruction. It should be noted that the Luftwaffe had tested the route and attacked the target over a number of days, but not as intensively as the seventy-four-plane raid of 28 April 1942, which was to be a two-hour spectacular with the intention of creating a fire storm.

It would have come as no surprise to either side that the resulting ninety dead and injured and broken buildings did nothing to dent the civilian resolution to survive and win through. The people of York buried their dead, tidied up and got on with the job; just as they always had over the centuries. There had been worse events in York's history; the entire city had burnt more than once, including the Minster, which every time had risen again more glorious than before.

The Baedeker Raid on York

www.bbc.co.uk/ww2peopleswar/stories/73/a2228573.shtml

The author, having studied the raid, considers that York got off very lightly; mainly as a result of the apparent markers laid down by the first wave of bombers. The most noticeable mass from the air other than the Minster was the railway station and any bomber pilot knows instinctively to go for strategic targets even if the instruction is for civilian structures. As a result of attacking the railway station, associated carriage works and loco sheds the raid did more damage outside the ancient part of the city than in it. A string of bombs in the Fulford area to the south-east and incendiary and high-explosive bombs south of the Ouse seemed to have been markers for the station, drawing much of the attack out of the centre. As there was no effective air defence, the Luftwaffe roughed up the city with low-level straffing. In general the old city came off relatively well, with the majority of the bombs hitting the north-west, beyond Bootham Bar.

The author has a suspicion that the Luftwaffe pilots were less than enamoured with their orders. The German war machine that had raged across Europe a couple of months previously was now finding the tide turning against it; the British were fighting back. Indeed, the Luftwaffe was shortly to be needed in Africa and, after defeat there, on the Eastern Front where it was all going terribly wrong. Thus this futile gesture was a last gasp.

The British took up the gauntlet and began a furious campaign of annihilation of German cities on a scale that the Germans could never have imagined.

Fortunately, the insanity came to an end and life for all flourished again; the great cities of Europe swept away the rubble and built again. As York remarkably survived in a better state than Exeter and Coventry, the city centre retained its unique character.

The walk starts at the Guildhall, a rather odd-looking building which shows signs of extension upon extension and different roofscapes – a feature especially noticeable from the river. It makes its presence felt in a solid and rooted manner. Its roof was its undoing: so difficult was it to clamber over and deal with incendiaries that it was a foregone conclusion that it would burn.

The core of the structure is fifteenth century and is worth a look; however, the incendiary bomb that hit the roof devastated the main structure. Old, dry timbers burn well and the hall was a shattered ruin until restored in the 1960s. It is a tribute to the restorers that the work doesn't attempt to hide itself but follows the same traditional line and attention to detail; it is not a studious copy, it is an evocation of craftsmanship doing homage to their forefathers by continuing in the tradition of good, solid work. The west window is a delight and allows the space to be well lit with natural light and, from shattered ruins; it has risen to shine out on York's public moments – an indoor space of great worth to the city.

The Guildhall nearly suffered another severe fire in 2007, when a lamp blew next to the wooden roof; fortunately it was quckly noticed and the fire brigade prevented a repeat of 1942.

The walker should take a while to enjoy the atmosphere and then head for the Mansion House.

The author considers the walker now well versed in traversing the city that such apparent flippancy of direction is more a genial test of the walker's ability to navigate the city with ease (and thus watch other visitors lost in maps) rather than the fact that he is in rather a hurry to head for the Yorkshire Terrier.

That, and the evening light takes his mind back to one of his evening strolls around the less well-known parts of the city centre.

The author has always enjoyed an adventure of whatever scale and he was accidentally trespassing (no doubt) round the back of the exhibition buildings one late afternoon, following his mind's eye. He was actually working on his theory for the position of the amphitheatre when he came across what appeared to be a pretty typical Second World War building – a very forlorn, lost sort of place that had been enclosed by all around it, yet no one had decided to remove it; it was simply attended by time and nature's hand.

There the discovery would have ended had it not been for the sound. As a child the author had a wind-up gramophone, rather a grand one, portable in a dark-blue case and sparkling chrome works. So the sound of a 78rpm record at the end of its play, with the regular hissing click every revolution, came straight back into his mind. The author mused for a moment that it was a mistake, that something else could make the noise, then the unmistakeable sound of the Jimmy Dorsey band and *María Elena*. The author decided to beat a retreat – further investigation of the hut seemed an intrusion on others' privacy. At this point the Yorkshire Terrier seemed a better prospect and it had got very cold all of a sudden. The past is sometimes better left where it is; someone enjoying a brief interlude from a world gone mad, whatever era the sound came from.

The buildings were actually constructed after the raid on York as a rest centre for RAF crews needing a bed for the night before heading back to their airfields or having a couple of days' leave in the city. Built on the ruins of part of the exhibition art gallery, it proved to be a comfortable billet and survived in a reasonable enough state to end its days as a venue for adult education classes.

During the air raid, the Mansion House was hit within seconds of the Guildhall, as part of the same string of incendiary bombs. The difference was that the bombs were dealt with and the fires extinguished; the Mansion House was thus available as a third line of defence for the communications system fighting the fires, the primary and secondary systems having been lost to the flames. The Mansion House, built to house the mayor and the focal point for pride in the corporation, was to play its greatest part in the history of York. The army installed temporary telephone lines as the bombs were still dropping and the fight to save the city was managed with great skill and no little courage, even as the Luftwaffe attempted to wipe York from the map.

York had expected a raid. It was common knowledge in the population that a tit-for-tat stage had been reached. However, the Germans had been repelled and any invasion plan of Britain was a thing of the past. Germany had turned on Russia, dividing its efforts, and thus savage sniping and attempts to isolate Britain by cutting its sea corridor was all Germany could manage.

Britain had been preparing for war since the mid-1930s and by its outbreak, unbeknown to the Germans, the country had a sophisticated wartime administration in place. Some of this is only slowly emerging from the dust of time in the twenty-first century, so secret and deep was the planning that it surprises archaeologists and historians alike.

One major question remains unanswered. The flying conditions were good, and yet the Germans were able to pound York for over an hour without any British fighters being sent to protect it. The author considers this particularly worthy of comment. With the use of radar and decoding of Enigma messages, the British High Command was fully aware of the Luftwaffe's movements. The author accepts that the Germans would have smelt a rat if the British were always waiting for them wherever they attacked and thus have changed their communications system; however, RAF Command seemed to decide to concentrate its fighters on coastal defence and protection of bomber squadrons and airfields associated with bombing campaigns. As if there was a conscious decision that these German raids could be absorbed as they were not doing serious damage to war production.

The walker should now proceed to Coney Street.

There is a very obvious clock in Coney Street; it makes sure the passer-by knows that they are late. It is not a shy clock that allows the walker to avoid it. St Martin's church seems to be attached to it, rather than the other way round.

St Martin's, one of the Norman churches of York, was hit by a high-explosive bomb and an incendiary. A large chunk of the church was destroyed in seconds, and was still a pile of rubble at the start of the 1960s. Fortunately, the great fifteenth-century west window was removed as a precaution in 1940 – a wise decision indeed. It now stands resplendent in a reduced but no less calming atmosphere – if anything it is a more intimate place and rightly a place for remembrance.

The walker should now head for Bootham Bar and Exhibition Square, no doubt stopping for another view of the Minster and perhaps some light refreshment – coffee perhaps? The smell of freshly ground coffee beans has a magnetic effect and retailers know it. York has a number of very fine coffee sellers and blenders – some also sell tea.

The walker will have noticed on previous walks (at least the author hopes so) the King's Manor, which has not been mentioned before. This is not a case of forgetfulness on the part of the author, but more a case of finding an appropriate spot to fit it in. King's Manor, sitting in its own grounds with

Kings Manor

145

elaborate gates and refined ancient elegance, was originally the property of the abbots of St Mary's abbey; thus, by way of a king changing a country's religion for financial gain, it became the property of Henry VIII and the seat of government, appropriately known as the Council for the North, until it was finally abolished in 1641.

Up to that point royalty and government ministers would use the spot as a stopping-off point; so the walls will have heard much intrigue, plots and political chicanery over the centuries. No doubt they still do as the building is occupied by the University of York Archaeology Department. At the time of the air raid the manor housed a school for the blind.

An incendiary bomb and the resultant fires seriously damaged the exhibition buildings next door and the manor took serious damage, with the Bootham Bar and crescent area a sea of flames. The walker should consider how different the view is today, with the fountain and the tourist buses clamouring for business, compared to that of the National Fire Service (NFS) fire engines, pumps and personnel fighting the flames attempting to consume the crescent. The whole city was filled with a mixture of burnt oak timbers and burnt toffee smoke as the old Rowntrees warehouse on North Street spewed out flames from the sugar fizzing within.

Fortunately, though the water mains pressure in the city had been disrupted, the Ouse came to the city's rescue and by the great efforts of the NFS, a series of hoses and pumps could supply the fire fighters with a sound supply, but not fast enough to save the Guildhall. The efforts of the NFS, staff of the North Eastern Railway, Civil Defence, ARPS and the people of York fought a valiant fight and, not without loss, won through.

The author knows how difficult the task was for the NFS: for a short while, when much younger, he helped to raise funds for the Fire Fighters Charity by taking part in demonstrations of NFS fire-fighting techniques. This meant the full, bulky uniform, bouncing around on a wooden bench on the back of a Bedford K2 fire engine and hauling incredibly heavy portable pumps into place and then leaning against the force of the water surging through the hose – no easy matter. Add to this bombs dropping all around and it just goes to prove that there were thousands of unsung heroes that history has all but forgotten.

Please support the fire fighters of today: www.firefighterscharity.org.uk.

Back to the attempted destruction of York; the fires are still raging in the crescent. The walker will have noted the general direction of the raid: whilst bombs were dropped near the Minster, the opportunity for a real firestorm at the Shambles seems to have been lost, as if the Luftwaffe overshot the ancient city and instead went for the later Victorian part of the town. The author

wonders if this was not deliberate on the part of the air crews. Whilst they flew low enough to use machine guns to smash plate-glass windows, the desire to smash the railway station and the loco works and junction would to them be a far more legitimate target. If the centre of the Shambles had been hit York would probably look very different today.

Consider the Luftwaffe's perspective on this, having successfully quelled all of mainland Europe with astonishing speed, things had been on the up. Then things turned nasty, the RAF with superior intelligence and radar stopped them. A close-run thing, but the Luftwaffe was diverted, which found them looking at the Mediterranean, planning for an eastern front with still having Britain to quell at the same time. The concentrated effort, so successful up to the Battle of Britain, waned and air crews found themselves being ordered to bomb historic sites rather than oil terminals. Architectural destruction isn't what the Luftwaffe was about; devastating industrial centres such as Glasgow, Coventry, Birmingham, Plymouth and Southampton would come higher on the list of priorities, with the crews having to risk their lives.

The walker should head directly to York railway station and look for the bus stand for services to Whitby, Scarborough and Bridlington (840, 843 and 845). Ask for a return ticket to Eden Camp. The best stop, should the driver not know it, is Railway Street, Malton.

The walker may travel by rail should they wish. The reason the author suggests travelling by bus is to get a top-deck seat and enjoy the splendid views.

The walker can, of course, travel by bus and return by train, or vice versa. Taxis are also not hard to find in Malton and for those wishing to walk it is roughly 30 minutes across the river and right on to Old Maltongate, which becomes Town Street; then under the A64, left on to Edenhouse Road and left again on to Pickering Road. In this case it's definitely faster by taxi and the A64 is busy and noisy.

The stations, bus and train, are across the Derwent and thus are not in Malton at all, a feature of railway stations in the UK with names that suit purpose rather than the actual fact. Canterbury Road on the old East Kent Railway was at least 20 miles from Canterbury and Bodmin Road is nowhere near Bodmin. At least Norton-on-Derwent is part of Malton and always has been.

Take a moment to look at Malton: a Roman settlement of some considerable note, grand houses, part of the *vicus* to Derventio (archaeological scholars may note this is the same name as the site at Papcastle in Cumbria – these things happen, there being more than one oak tree wood (for that is the translation) in Britannia, leading to a certain amount of duplication).

WALK 9

The Roman fort appears to have been the residence of cavalry units and the land between York and Malton suits not only the feeding of humans but bovines as well. There are suggestions that horse breeding has always been at the heart of the area, including pre-Roman tribal activity in the sport of people with more money than sense.

If the walker makes enough time Malton should be viewed and enjoyed, there being some excellent cafés and a few good pubs. It has characteristics of York, so take time to study the architecture. The market is on Saturday.

Eden Camp is a must see and a remarkable survivor.

Eden Camp
www.edencamp.co.uk

The walker should spend at least two and a half hours here as there is plenty to see and experience. At certain times of year it can be a very busy spot and it is very popular with school parties.

The author first visited with a lively school party some years ago; he was initially rather wary of what he was going to see – a wartime theme park slightly jarring with the reality of war. However, he found it a well-balanced and informative experience with some of the exhibits and experiences genuinely some of the best he has ever seen.

Eden Camp is part of the *Götterdämmerung* for the Nazi cause: a barbed-wire enclosure where German military personnel waited in relative comfort for the whole horrendous opera of death to come to a crashing end, with parts of Germany reduced to a worse state than York and most British cities.

To the author it seemed only right to show action and reaction in the history of York; this is a rare opportunity. In all the earlier destructions and damage all the perpetrators other than the leaders are anonymous to history. Eden Camp offers the faces and names, and they turn out to be no different from ourselves.

The raid on York took place at night; in the raid at least five schools were badly damaged, some to the point of destruction. However, the cost to York could have been much higher as the schools were empty; thus its future survived to cheer the fact there was no school in the morning and there was a day or two of collecting shrapnel and cartridge cases before the work of patching up and merging schools could commence, which would inevitably lead to the odd bloodied nose as the schoolyard 'bundle' between rival gangs would work out who ruled the roost.

The walker will probably come away from Eden Camp with the stench of submarine in the nose. It is a great place to visit and those leaving will definitely have a different impression of the Second World War than they had when they arrived.

Whichever means of transport the walker decides upon to return to York, the view on the way is the thing. A trip into the city is the only way to truly experience its impact. The city has a strong presence, not the suburbs that cling to its ring road; it is the Minster that truly stands out, rising majestically out of the plain as a beacon over the centuries – which is exactly what it is.

York; there is a definite sense of arrival.

The author considered long and hard regarding this particular day. He nearly didn't write it, as he has no desire to glamorise destruction, especially when there are people alive that can remember it and all that goes with such events, but York has been battered many times. The city is its people; stone can last many thousands of years, but we are flesh that breaks and turns to dust in moments. Yet it is this fragile form that sets the stones one upon another. There is blood, sweat, fear, death and dreams in the stone and this is as close to a destructive event in York's turmoil the walker will get.

The author refuses to end on a dismal note so suggests the walker heads for Betty's Tea Rooms on St Helen's Square.

▌Betty's Tea Rooms
www.bettys.co.uk/bettys_york.aspx

The walker will note the author is sending them to a tea room, which was a favourite location for service personnel during the war years, especially as it had, quite unusually, a licence to serve alcohol and was known as the Dive and the Briefing Room. Bomber Command spent much of their spare time in York and Betty's was a magnet for the airmen.

Spam fritters are not on the menu anymore, which is a pity as the author likes a Spam fritter and thinks the walker should have the chance to enjoy such a dish, but it is appropriate to end the day here.

Enjoy the afternoon tea; if you are visiting in summer there may well be a few others trying to do the same thing.

WALK 9

THE BIGGEST CHALLENGE OF ALL – YOUR OWN

- Starting time: 9 a.m.
- Explore! Make this one up for yourself
- Be part of the fabric and history of York
- The walker has much to see and experience

The author cannot cover everything in this guide, nor did he intend too; the purpose was to give an insight, just to draw the walker in. The author knows the walker has no choice but to return again and again: York has entered the bloodstream evoking an inner desire to wander around a city that slowly reveals itself; not without effort, but it will.

The walker is a part of the history of the city, perhaps this time will be looked back at as the age of tourism. New forums and temples have appeared for the citizens a short bus ride from the ancient walls; Monks Foss and Clifton Moor fulfil the desires.

The author hopes to see you – you might even see him. He's normally lurking in the darkest corner of any York pub with a guzzler in his hand, watching the world go by or looking down from his lofty perch at the throng, letting the coffee tempt him down to the street to walk through the walls and into the fabric of the place to worlds long gone but not forgotten.

The possible Anglian tower – the jury's out!

Here are some puzzling destinations and views in no particular order to keep the walker busy for the day:

- **Palm Sunday, 18 March 1190**
- **William Fitzherbert**
- **Mad Alice**
- **Photo opportunity: High Petergate to Precentor's Court**
- **Bedern Arch**
- **If betting, head for the site of the gallows**
- **William Etty**
- **The Brimstone House, the King's Fishpond**
- **Peasholme Green for some evening music and refreshment**

That should keep you busy for a day or two or, more likely as the city takes a hold, a lifetime. Once drawn in there really is no escape from the place.

The author looks down, the tables are being stowed away for the night; a brief lull in the city as many are heading for dinner or simply crashing out for a few hours after a heavy retail experience before a night out in a lively spot – no shortage of those south of the river.

York eventide

The Roman soldier is damping down the fire next to his tent; the trader is locking his shop; the monk is heading to prayer; and the musicians are preparing for a powder-strewn night in the Assembly Rooms.

York continues upon its eternal way.

The author wishes you a goodnight. May your way be an intriguing one, full of adventures and joy in the discovery.

See you soon.

Cheers!

USEFUL LIST

Emergency services
police, ambulance, fire, dial 999

North Yorkshire Police
Fulford Rd
York YO10 4BY
Tel: 0845 606 0247
Tel: 01904 631321

York Teaching Hospital NHS Foundation Trust
The York Hospital
Wigginton Road
York YO31 8HE
Tel: 01904 631 313

York Medical Group
York Medical Group Surgeries

Acomb
199 Acomb Road
York YO24 4HD
Tel: 01904 342 999

Monkgate
35 Monkgate
York YO31 7PB
Tel: 01904 342 989

Woodthorpe
40 Moorcroft Road
York YO24 2RQ
Tel: 01904 706881

University
York St John University
Lord Mayor's Walk
York YO31 7EX
Tel: 01904 724775

Dental Emergency
NHS York: 01904 725 422
NHS Direct Dental Helpline: 0845 600 3249

24-hour Pharmacy
Unit 7 Monks Cross
York YO32 9LF
Tel: 01904 6563602

Lost Property
Tel: 01904 551 677

Samaritans
89 Nunnery Lane
York, YO23 1AH
Tel: 01904 655 888

Taxi Companies
Station Taxis Ltd
Tel: 01653 696 969
Ryedale Taxis
Tel: 01653 600 026
121 Taxis
Tel: 01653 690 121
D.C. Cars
Tel: 01653 693 003abbey, 30, 59, 68, 76, 88, 91, 106, 146

INDEX